CHRISTIAN HEROES: THEN & NOW

C.T. STUDD

No Retreat

CHRISTIAN HEROES: THEN & NOW

C.T. STUDD

No Retreat

JANET & GEOFF BENGE

YWAM PUBLISHING
P.O. BOX 55787 SEATTLE, WA 98155

YWAM Publishing is the publishing ministry of Youth With A Mission (YWAM), an international missionary organization of Christians from many denominations dedicated to presenting Jesus Christ to this generation. To this end, YWAM has focused its efforts in three main areas: (1) training and equipping believers for their part in fulfilling the Great Commission (Matthew 28:19), (2) personal evangelism, and (3) mercy ministry (medical and relief work).

To learn more about our books and materials, call (425) 771-1153 or (800) 922-2143 or email books@ywampublishing.com. Visit us online at www.ywampublishing.com.

C.T. Studd: No Retreat

Published by YWAM Publishing
a ministry of Youth With A Mission
P.O. Box 55787, Seattle, WA 98155-0787

Library of Congress Cataloging-in-Publication Data
Benge, Janet, 1958–
C.T. Studd : no retreat / Janet & Geoff Benge.
p. cm. — (Christian heroes, then & now)
Includes bibliographical references.
ISBN 1-57658-288-4
1. Studd, C. T. (Charles Thomas), 1860–1931—Juvenile literature.
2. Missionaries—England—Biography—Juvenile literature.
3. Missionaries—Biography—Juvenile literature. I. Benge, Geoff, 1954–
II. Title. III. Series.
BV3705.S78B46 2005
266′.0092—dc22 2005000850

ISBN 978-1-57658-288-6 (paperback)
ISBN 978-1-57658-611-2 (e-book)

Sixth printing 2026

Printed in the United States of America

Christian Heroes: Then & Now

Adoniram Judson
Albert Schweitzer
Amy Carmichael
Betty Greene
Brother Andrew
Cameron Townsend
Charles Mulli
Clarence Jones
Corrie ten Boom
Count Zinzendorf
C. S. Lewis
C. T. Studd
David Bussau
David Livingstone
Dietrich Bonhoeffer
D. L. Moody
Elisabeth Elliot
Eric Liddell
Florence Young
Francis Asbury
George Müller
Gladys Aylward
Helen Roseveare
Hudson Taylor
Ida Scudder
Isobel Kuhn
Jacob DeShazer
Jim Elliot
John Flynn
John Newton
John Wesley
John Williams
Jonathan Goforth
Klaus-Dieter John
Lillian Trasher
Loren Cunningham
Lottie Moon
Mary Slessor
Mildred Cable
Nate Saint
Norman Grubb
Paul Brand
Rachel Saint
Richard Wurmbrand
Rowland Bingham
Samuel Zwemer
Sundar Singh
Wilfred Grenfell
William Booth
William Carey

Available in paperback, e-book, and audiobook formats. Unit study curriculum guides are available for select biographies.

www.YWAMpublishing.com

Africa

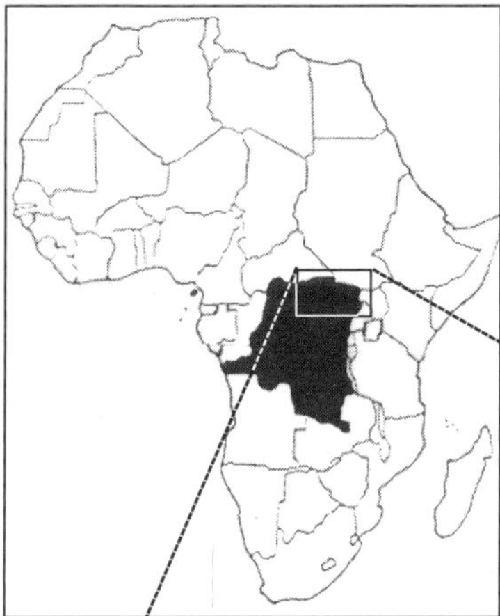

Northwestern Belgian Congo (Dem. Rep. of the Congo)

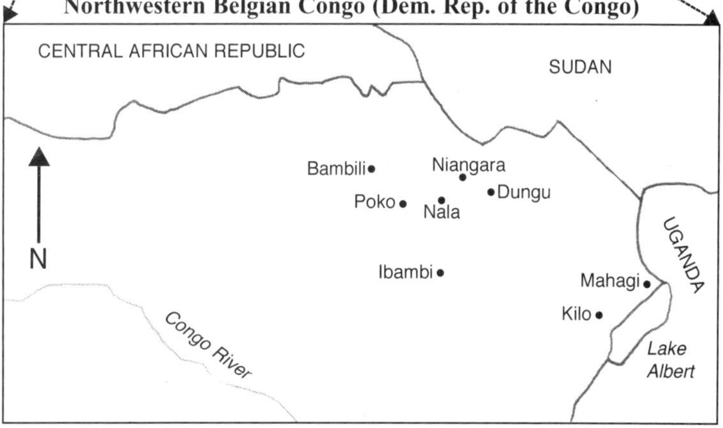

Contents

1. Lost 11
2. A Religious Fanatic 15
3. A Star Cricketer. 27
4. The Cambridge Seven 37
5. China at Last 49
6. He Had Never Met a Woman Like Priscilla 63
7. Foreign Devils 75
8. India 89
9. For Want of a Christian Missionary 101
10. Africa at Last 113
11. Lunch with Cannibals 123
12. In the Heart of Africa. 133
13. Bwana Mukubwa 145
14. God Is to Be Found in Nala 159
15. A New Venture. 169
16. No Chocolate Soldier 181

Bibliography 189

Chapter 1

Lost

We're lost," C.T. Studd said, shaking his head.

C.T. and his traveling companion, Alfred Buxton, had been trying to find their way back to the trail through the dense African jungle, but all they had succeeded in doing was walking in circles until they were now totally disoriented.

"And hungry," Alfred added.

The men's porters, from whom they had become separated, were carrying all of their food and supplies.

The two Englishmen walked on a little farther and came upon a small clearing. They emerged from the sunless gloom of the jungle into the bright sunlight of the clearing. C.T. studied the sky above, searching for a cloud, a migrating bird, anything that might help him get his bearings.

"You know, this is the area where that elephant hunter we heard about was shot and killed with a poison dart," Alfred said.

A shiver ran up C.T.'s spine at the thought. "I know," he replied, "and I have a strange feeling we're being watched right now."

"Yes, I know what you mean," Alfred said. "Do you have any idea which direction we should head to get out of here?"

Before C.T. could answer, the men heard a rustle in the jungle behind them. They spun around to see an African man emerge from the dense foliage. The man was naked except for the tattered shirt that he wore. C.T.'s and Alfred's eyes were drawn to the bow and arrows the man held in his left hand. The man smiled, revealing teeth that had been filed to sharp points.

"The teeth, a sure sign he is a cannibal," C.T. said.

It was then that C.T. noticed the plaited basket the man was carrying in his right hand. The basket was filled with sweet potatoes and cobs of maize. The man was still smiling, and sensing that he meant them no harm, C.T. smiled back and pointed to the basket. He then patted his stomach to indicate he was hungry, and the man seemed to understand what he was saying. He walked forward and handed several cobs of maize and some sweet potatoes to C.T.

"Thank you," C.T. said as he took them, though he knew the man had no idea what he was saying.

C.T. did not want to just take the vegetables from the man. He wanted to pay him for them, but neither he nor Alfred had any money on him. C.T. wondered what he could give the man in return. It was then that he noticed the buttons on his pants. "Why do pants have so many buttons?" he asked Alfred.

Alfred gave him a bewildered look, unsure what such a question had to do with their present situation.

"I'll tell you," C.T. continued. "To give to undressed cannibals." With that he tore six buttons off his pants and gave them to the man.

A broad smile spread across the man's face, and his sharpened teeth glistened in the sunlight. Then, suddenly, the man beckoned for the two missionaries to follow him as he set off into the jungle. C.T. and Alfred looked at each other and then followed him.

An hour later they came to another clearing, in which was located a small village.

"Do you think this might be a trap and they're going to kill us and eat us?" Alfred asked as they approached the village.

"No, I don't think so," C.T. said in a calm voice. "Look at us. We're too lean and lanky and tough for them to try to cook and eat. There are more tender and appetizing animals to eat in the jungle."

The man guided them to sit beside a fire near one of the grass huts. Once he was sure they were comfortable, he placed the sweet potatoes and ears of maize into the embers of the fire. Half an hour later he pulled the vegetables from the embers and served them to C.T. and Alfred. He brought some cooked meat from inside the hut and served it to them as well. The two famished men began to gobble down the meat and vegetables.

"The sweet potatoes and maize are cooked perfectly," Alfred said as they ate. "And the meat was tender and tasty. I wonder what animal it is from."

"In a cannibal village that might not be a good thing to inquire about," C.T. said dryly.

Their host sat smiling as the men ate.

"Imagine if people in England could see us now," Alfred said.

"Yes. Most of them could scarcely believe it," C.T. replied.

As C.T. chewed on an ear of maize, he thought more about Alfred's remark. What would people in England think? C.T. had been raised in a privileged family. He had attended the best schools in England. He had been the top cricket player in the country. Thousands of people used to come to watch him play. Could those who came to watch him have ever imagined that their cricket hero would one day be sitting in the middle of a dense jungle in the heart of Africa having lunch with cannibals? C.T. could scarcely believe it himself. His life had certainly taken a different turn from what he had ever imagined it would be. Indeed, if people back home could see him now!

Chapter 2

A Religious Fanatic

In the quadrangle of Eton College, a preparatory high school, C.T. Studd stood talking with several of his friends.

"Amazing. All three of you in the first eleven!" Cecil Polhill-Turner exclaimed. "Look out for those Studd boys! Eighteen seventy-seven is going to be our best year yet. We are going to beat Harrow!"

C.T. laughed. "It will take more than the three of us to make a great cricket team. But we are going to do our best. I can hardly wait to tell Father."

Edward Studd would be the proudest man in England, C.T. was sure of that. His three oldest sons, nineteen-year-old Kynaston, or Kinny for short, eighteen-year-old George, and seventeen-year-old Charles Thomas, whom everyone called C.T., were on Eton College's premier cricket team all at the same time. Their father loved any kind of sport, but especially cricket and horse racing. One of his horses, named Salamander, had even won the Grand National Championship in England.

"Here comes Kinny now," Cecil said with admiration.

Kinny Studd strolled toward the group with the air of someone who had just learned he was to be the captain of the most popular sports team on campus. In his hand he held a letter.

"Hello," he said, ruffling his younger brother's hair. "I have a letter from Father. He says he wants to meet the three of us in London this weekend. Can you make it?"

C.T. nodded. "Does he say what he wants us for?"

"No," Kinny replied. "I expect he wants to celebrate with us, probably go to the theater or hear the Christy Minstrels, something like that."

"Sounds great," C.T. said. "I wonder who told him the great news."

The boys talked for a few more minutes before going their separate ways. C.T. went back to the rooms he shared with his two brothers. His first job was to make sure that their servant would have his Sunday clothes ready for the weekend excursion. The Studds were among the wealthiest families in England, and Mr. Studd liked his sons to look the part at all times.

Saturday arrived, and the three brothers climbed aboard a train for Paddington Station, where they had agreed to meet their father, who was waiting for them on the platform. Although he was fifty-six years old, Edward Studd looked sprightlier than ever, waving at the boys as soon as he spotted them through the carriage window.

After their father had greeted each of his sons, C.T. spoke up. "So where are you taking us?" he asked.

"Oh, didn't I mention it in the letter? We are off to Drury Lane to hear a very special performance. I am sure you will all find it fascinating."

"Why? What are you taking us to see?" Kinny asked, but their father simply beckoned for them to follow him through the crowded station and out to a waiting carriage.

As they walked, C.T. tried to think of who might have captivated his father's attention so completely that he forgot to congratulate his sons for making the first eleven cricket team.

As the carriage rounded a corner near Drury Lane, C.T. froze in shock. Huge placards announced, "Come and hear Dwight L. Moody and Ira Sankey."

George leaned over and whispered to C.T. "I can't believe it. Do you think Father has gone religious on us?"

As if to answer the question, Edward Studd cleared his throat and spoke. "I have something very important to tell you. Since we were together last summer, I have experienced a change of heart. My dear friend Mr. Vincent and his family came to stay, and I found him quite different from the man

I had known in India for so many years. He invited me along here to the Drury Lane Theater to hear two Americans, Moody and Sankey. I was not keen to go, but I had said he could name the entertainment for the evening, and that is where he wanted to go. At any rate, we went along, and I must say, Moody spoke more sense than any man that I have ever heard. I am not ashamed to say I went back night after night until I was soundly converted."

A stunned silence followed, until finally Kinny spoke up. "Converted? You mean converted into... into a religious fanatic?"

C.T. looked at his father and saw a huge grin spread over his face.

"Just wait until you experience it too!" Mr. Studd replied. "There is nothing in the world compared to knowing Jesus Christ. Why, since I have taken him into my heart, my whole life has changed. My passion for horse racing is gone, and I barely have time to shoot anymore. You'd hardly know the house, either. I have cleared out the large hall and brought in chairs and benches. All sorts of people—merchants, business associates, servants—everyone comes to hear preachers at the house. It is marvelous!"

"And what about Mother?" George choked.

"She's been converted too and is right behind me. I have never felt such joy in my whole life! Jesus Christ is the answer, boys. That I am sure of. He is the answer to all of life's questions."

C.T. looked down at the carriage seat. He hardly dared to look up in case he caught the eye of one of his brothers. How would they stop from laughing out loud if that happened? His father, the shrewd businessman who had made a fortune in India as a young man and then returned to England to live a life of ease, was now a fanatical Christian? It was almost too much to take in. C.T. wished he'd had some warning to get used to the idea.

"Come along," Mr. Studd said encouragingly as the carriage came to a stop outside the theater. "Come and hear Moody for yourself. Then I'll take you back to the house for dinner, and you can ask me all the questions you want."

The house Edward Studd referred to was located in the fashionable area of Hyde Park Garden. Mr. Studd had bought the place some years before so that he would have somewhere to stay when he came to London to buy and bet on horses. C.T. would have given just about anything to be at the house right then, swapping cricket stories with his father. Instead he and his brothers followed their father into the hall. The crowd was already singing hymns, none of which were familiar to C.T. Like all well-brought-up English boys, C.T. had been to church every Sunday of his life, but these were not the traditional Anglican hymns he was used to.

The hymns were not the only things foreign to C.T. When Dwight Moody took the platform and started to speak, C.T. realized he had never before heard anyone preach with so much enthusiasm or conviction. He listened carefully to Dwight L. Moody, but he found it hard to imagine why his father found it all so exciting. Despite Moody's enthusiasm and conviction, it still sounded like religious mumbo jumbo to C.T., who was eager to be out of the strange environment he found himself in.

Once the service was over, Mr. Studd summoned a carriage to take them all back to the house for dinner. The conversation around the meal was rather one-sided. All three brothers had the same reaction to their father's new religious exuberance—they did not want to know anything more about it.

In his wildest dreams, C.T. could not have imagined this moment. As they ate dessert, Mr. Studd explained that he was going to keep four horses, one for himself and one for each of the boys, and sell the rest. He had lost interest in breeding racehorses or gambling on them.

"I talked to Moody about it," Mr. Studd said happily, "and he told me that God would give me souls and that as soon as I had won a soul, I wouldn't care about anything else. And you know what, boys? He was right. As soon as I won my first convert, I couldn't care less about racing or making money. Isn't that wonderful?"

No one answered.

The following week the three Studd brothers were glad to attend chapel at Eton. It all seemed so normal after their strange religious encounter of the weekend before.

As the weeks went by, C.T. tried to forget about his father's conversion, but in the back of his mind he knew he would have to go home for the summer and face the religious meetings that his father held at the family's estate in Tedworth every weekend. Slowly, as news spread around Eton that Mr. Studd had been converted, many of the other boys came to offer C.T. their sympathy. They could not imagine anything worse than having an evangelical father.

Thankfully, C.T. and his brothers had their cricket careers to concentrate on. Not only did Eton manage to beat its archrival, Harrow, with them on the team, but in one game Kinny scored 52 runs, C.T. 53, and George 54. It was a rare achievement.

Finally summer arrived, and C.T. and his brothers packed their belongings into trunks and headed for home. Tedworth House, with its huge, white columns and curved, two-story exterior, looked just as imposing as ever, but for the first time, C.T. was nervous about going inside. Sure enough, just as his father had said, the marble-floored dance hall had been outfitted with chairs and benches, and hymnals and Bibles were piled high by the door.

Mr. and Mrs. Studd warmly greeted their returning sons while C.T.'s three younger brothers, Peter, Herbert, and Reginald, and his little sister, Dora, all crowded around to welcome the "big" boys home. The younger siblings talked about some of the events they had planned for the summer—picnics, cricket matches, and hunting parties—but most of all they talked about the weekend meetings that drew several hundred people. C.T. cringed as he thought of his childhood friends and their families being invited to such meetings.

Things did not go well from the start. C.T. did his best to avoid his father. Whenever they were together, Edward Studd turned the conversation to religious matters and often asked C.T. if he wanted to get saved. He even came into his son's room at night to sit on the end of the bed and explain why becoming a Christian would be a wonderful thing to do. This was all too much for C.T., who felt hounded in his own house. Often when he heard his father coming into his room at night, he pretended to be asleep, and he sneaked around the house, making sure that his father was not already in a room before he entered it.

The weekends were the worst of all, when the house was filled with Christians. The visitors sang, not just in the meetings but all the time. Sometimes C.T. would hear them singing and even praying in the garden or the dining room. And they talked of little else besides Jesus Christ, until C.T. and his brothers could not stand it anymore.

When a Mr. Weatherby, a thin, humorless man, arrived to preach for the weekend, it was the last straw. The three older Studd boys decided it was time to do something. Old Weatherby, as they called him, had to go!

"I've seen Old Weatherby on a horse," C.T. confided in his brothers on Saturday morning, "and he's not much of a horseman. Let's ask him if he wants to come with us for a leisurely ride. He can ride Father's horse. We'll start off slowly and then set our horses to race. Father's horse won't be able to resist, and we'll see how long Old Weatherby can stay in the saddle!"

Everything went as planned. Kinny, George, and C.T. trotted their horses out of the stable and waited for Mr. Weatherby to mount the fourth horse. Riding was in C.T.'s blood. In fact, all of the Studd boys had been on horses for as long as they could remember. Their mother had dressed them in matching red riding outfits, and their father had tied them to the saddle and taught each boy to jump before his sixth birthday.

Soon the four were out in the fields around Tedworth House. It was a scene C.T. loved, especially the sheep grazing lazily between the hedgerows. The three boys started out slowly, and then with a raised eyebrow, C.T. signaled for them to canter. He looked behind him to see Mr. Weatherby's startled look as his horse took off at a gallop after the other three horses. Mr. Weatherby clung to the saddle, a grim look of determination fixed across his face.

The boys' horses raced faster, jumping effortlessly over a gate, but the preacher stayed right behind them. They tried another jump and then another, but nothing would unseat Old Weatherby. Eventually the boys slowed their horses to a trot, and Mr. Weatherby came up beside them. C.T. expected him to be angry, but he merely said, "Nice day for a ride, isn't it?" and smiled.

For the first time, C.T. felt a little ashamed of the trick he and his brothers had played on their father's guest. But the feeling did not last long, and C.T.

spent the rest of the day avoiding Mr. Weatherby, until toward evening he rounded a corner of the house and came face-to-face with the man.

"Can you spare me a few minutes, C.T.?" Mr. Weatherby asked.

The last thing C.T. wanted to do was to be alone with Old Weatherby, but he did feel he owed him a little courtesy after the trick they had played on him that morning.

"I have a little time," he replied.

"Good," Mr. Weatherby replied. "Why don't we sit down on these lawn chairs and have a chat."

C.T. obediently sat down, and Old Weatherby started in right away.

"Are you a Christian, C.T.?" the preacher asked.

C.T. felt cornered. He did not know what to say. After a long silence he did the best he could. "I am not what *you* would call a Christian. But I have believed in Jesus Christ since I was knee-high." He tried not to look Mr. Weatherby in the eye. "And, of course, I believe in the church, too," he added, hoping that that would be enough to satisfy the man, but it was not.

"Look here, C.T. God so loved the world that He gave His only begotten Son, that whosoever believeth on Him should not perish but have everlasting life. Now, do you believe Jesus Christ died?"

C.T. hesitated for a moment. He did not want to get caught in a trap, but he decided to answer as honestly as he could.

"Yes, I believe that," he said.

"Well, do you believe He died for you?" Mr. Weatherby persisted.

"Yes," C.T. mumbled.

"Good. And do you believe the other half of the verse, that you shall have everlasting life?"

"Not exactly," C.T. answered. "I find that very hard to believe."

"Isn't it inconsistent to believe one half of the verse and not the other?" Mr. Weatherby asked.

"I suppose so," C.T. replied.

"And are you always going to be inconsistent in what you believe?"

"Not always," C.T. said. "One day I will work it all out."

"Why not now? Today?" Mr. Weatherby pressed.

As C.T. thought about it, he realized it was a reasonable question. How could he believe one half of a Bible verse and not the other? He sighed and then spoke. "I suppose I am ready to be consistent in what I believe."

"Wonderful! Don't you see that eternal life is a gift? And if someone offers you a gift at Christmastime, what do you do?" Mr. Weatherby did not wait for an answer; he patted C.T. on the back and continued. "You take it and say thank you, don't you? Now why don't you take the gift of eternal life and say thank you to God for it?"

Put that way, it made sense to C.T., and since no one else was around, C.T. got down on his knees and mumbled his thanks to God.

Much to his surprise, when he got to his feet, C.T.

felt quite different—joyful and light. Mr. Weatherby talked to him for a few more minutes about praying and reading his Bible regularly, and then the two of them parted.

As C.T. walked off in the direction of the cricket pitch, he decided two things. First, it was not so awful being a Christian after all, and second, he was not going to tell a soul about what he had done.

Chapter 3

A Star Cricketer

Now back at Eton, C.T. Studd sat at the breakfast table with his two brothers. C.T. had kept his promise to himself not to tell anyone that he had become a Christian, with one exception. When he got back to Eton, he had written a letter he had marked "Private" to his father, explaining his conversion. He hoped this would make his father happy.

That morning the servant brought in a letter and handed it to Kinny. The letter was addressed to all three boys, and Kinny read it first. Without saying a word, he handed it to George, who in turn read it silently and then gave it to C.T.

As C.T. read the letter, he could hardly believe what it said. His father was congratulating each of the boys on becoming a Christian on the same day, each as the result of talking to Mr. Weatherby!

C.T. looked at his brothers, who seemed as shocked as he was. Evidently each of them had made the same decision not to tell anyone else what he had done.

"The cat's out of the bag now, isn't it?" Kinny laughed. "Did you mean it when you talked to Old Weatherby?"

"Yes," C.T. replied. "I just didn't want to make a public song and dance about it. You know how Father is about such things these days."

"I felt the same way," George agreed. "But I have been reading my Bible and praying every day, and I must say, chapel service has been making a great deal more sense to me."

"Me, too," Kinny said. "I can hardly believe it! I have been praying for both of you, and here you are already Christians."

The three boys talked through breakfast, marveling at how each of them had been converted on the same day after resisting it for nearly a year. They also decided to start a group Bible study with some of their close friends.

Things went smoothly for C.T. that year. He dedicated most of his time to cricket, but he did go to the Bible studies that Kinny led. And things were easier at home now that Mr. Studd was satisfied that his boys were headed in the right direction.

At the end of the year, Kinny went off to Trinity College at Cambridge, and the following year George joined him, leaving C.T. alone at Eton, where he was named the captain of the first eleven cricket team.

During the 1879–1880 school year, C.T. threw himself into all kinds of sports. He was a natural athlete, and he felt that cross training would benefit his cricket game. He was particularly good at racquets and successfully represented Eton in this sport.

He was still living a "good life" as far as he could, but without his brothers' support, C.T. stopped going to Bible studies, and the joy he had once felt drifted away. But he was so busy he hardly noticed.

Then one day in November 1879 C.T. was called to the headmaster's office. As he knocked on the door, he wondered what could be so serious for him to be summoned from Latin class. He soon found out. His father was dead! The headmaster had already called a carriage to take C.T. home. It was almost too much for C.T. to take in. The last time he had seen him, his father was healthy and fit. All the way back to Tedworth House, C.T. wondered what could have possibly happened. Once he arrived home, he learned the details from his mother.

"It was so like your father," his mother began as she dabbed her tears with a handkerchief. "We were on our way to a mission meeting last night, and he suddenly stopped the carriage. He said he had forgotten to invite one of the grooms to come along with us. I tried to tell him that we could invite him to the next meeting, but he insisted that the carriage go on while he went back to the house. He would find the groom, and the two of them would ride to the meeting on horseback. He didn't make it to the meeting, and when I got home, I found him lying on the couch. Apparently he had run all the way home and broken a blood vessel in his leg. I called the doctor, of course, but there was little he could do, and your father died this morning."

C.T. put his arm around his mother, but he did not know what to say to comfort her.

The following day at the funeral service, the minister told the huge crowd that Mr. Studd had done more for God in the two years he had been a Christian than most Christians do in twenty years. However, it was the coachman who C.T. thought said it best. "When Mr. Studd became religious, we didn't know much about it except that though there was the same skin on the outside, there was a new man inside."

The family was thankful that Edward Studd had left a clearly worded will that allowed for each of his sons to inherit a large sum of money on his twenty-sixth birthday. As the oldest child, Kinny inherited the family estate, with the provision that his mother be allowed to live in the house at Hyde Park until her death.

Within a week of the funeral, C.T. was back in school to finish off his final year at Eton. He still had difficulty believing that his father was really dead. It had all happened so quickly.

Like his two older brothers, at the end of his time at Eton, C.T. enrolled at Trinity College, Cambridge, where he was immediately recognized for his potential as a great cricket player. In his freshman year he was given his cricket blue, an honor conferred on those who demonstrated great skill in the sport, and he played for the second eleven cricket team. His game continued to improve, and in his second year C.T. joined Kinny and George on the first eleven team.

The brothers made for an unstoppable combination. In one match the three of them made 249 of the 504 runs the Cambridge cricket team scored. C.T. turned out to be the most promising of the three brothers, and on another occasion he made 267 of the 362 runs scored.

In 1882 the three brothers were once again on the Cambridge cricket team. It was also the year the Australian cricket team made its third visit to England. The Australians fielded a particularly strong team, winning all their games in the run up to the test match with the English team.

Before the test match was played, the Australian team captain asked if they could play a game against the Cambridge first eleven. Most people, including the president of the Cambridge Cricket Club, thought that this was a terrible idea. If the Australians had beaten every team they had played so far, what would they do to a university team? If the Cambridge team agreed to the match, everyone was sure they would disgrace themselves playing against such a strong colonial side. Despite the misgivings, the Cambridge team agreed, and a match was scheduled.

It was a gloriously clear and sunny Monday when the two teams took the field for the match. A huge crowd had gathered to watch. The Australians batted first, and as the two opening batsmen began to score run after run, people were sure their worst fears would be realized—Cambridge would be soundly beaten by the Australians.

C.T., who was one of the opening bowlers for Cambridge, did his best to get the Australian batsmen out, but the opponents managed to hit nearly every ball he bowled to them. Then just as the situation seemed hopeless for Cambridge, one of the Australian batsmen swung at a ball bowled by C.T. However, he did not get his bat squarely on the ball, and the ball glanced sideways, where it was caught by one of the Cambridge fielders. The first Australian batsman was out. Now all Cambridge needed to do was get nine more batsmen out to end the inning. To everyone's surprise, this did not take very long, as one batsman after another was bowled out, leaving Australia with a paltry 139 runs for the inning.

Now it was Cambridge's turn to bat. Kinny and George batted first. Kinny was eventually bowled out and then two other Cambridge batsmen. It was then C.T.'s turn to bat. C.T. joined George on the pitch, and between them they scored most of Cambridge's runs.

The match continued on Tuesday, with an even larger crowd gathered to watch than the day before. Cambridge was eventually out for 266 runs, and

Australia began their second inning at bat. They scored 290 runs in the inning, leaving Cambridge 164 runs to score to win the match. Kinny and George were once again the leadoff batsmen, scoring 106 runs between them before George was bowled out. Finally it was C.T.'s turn to bat, and he scored fifteen runs not out, including the winning run. Cambridge had done what no one thought they could do—beat the formidable Australian team.

The authoritative book *Lillywhite's Cricket Record* summed up C.T.'s achievement this way: "Very few players have a finer style: brilliant leg hitting and driving, with a very hard wrist stroke in front of point, a real straight bat, and a resolute nerve to make together a batsman whose back bowlers are very glad to see."

Although C.T. was still only in his third year of college, he was ranked at the top of his sport, a young player who could outdo amateurs and professionals alike. Yet he was still surprised and delighted to be asked to be a member of the English National Cricket team to play the test match against Australia.

Critics ranked the team among one of England's finest, and twenty thousand people turned out at the Oval in London to witness the contest. It was a hard-fought match, and when it was all over, Australia had beaten England in cricket for the first time.

While the Australians celebrated, a gloom settled over many English cricket fans. After the match the *Sporting Times* newspaper printed an epitaph for English cricket:

> In Affectionate Remembrance
> of
> English Cricket,
> Which died at the Oval on
> 29th August, 1882,
> Deeply lamented by a large circle of
> Sorrowing Friends and
> Acquaintances.
> R.I.P.
> N.B. The body will be cremated and
> the ashes taken to Australia

Despite the loss, C.T. Studd found himself a household name in England. Back at Cambridge everyone offered him congratulations and invited him to the most popular parties. And then that winter C.T. and George were picked for the English team going to Australia to play a series of test matches.

On his first trip outside of England, C.T. enjoyed every minute of the long ship voyage to Australia. Once there, the English and the Australians played three cricket matches, and with some brilliant playing on the part of C.T., the English won two of them.

As the English team prepared to board ship for the trip home, a group of Melbourne women arrived to make a presentation. They had put some ashes in a small silver urn, which they gave to the captain of the team. As they turned the urn over, they announced that the English had won back their "ashes," but they had better watch out next time, as the Australians fully intended to win the ashes back again.

Everyone cheered as the urn was brought aboard the ship, and a newspaper reporter telegraphed news of it to England. When the ship docked in London, a crowd was waiting for the team, calling to see the hard-won ashes. It was the beginning of a long tradition between Australia and England of playing for possession of the ashes.

By now it was impossible for C.T. to go anywhere without being recognized and asked for his autograph. C.T. captained the Cambridge first eleven in his final year, and the team enjoyed another winning season.

The *Cricketing Annual* summed up C.T.'s performance by saying, "Mr. C.T. Studd must for the second year in succession be accorded the premier position as an all-round cricketer, and some years have elapsed since the post has been filled by a player so excellent in all the three departments of the game. His batting especially has been of the highest class."

After C.T. passed his final exams, earning a B.A. degree, he left college for London. He planned to enjoy himself there and prepare for another season with the English cricket team. Indeed, he intended to play for the team for the next several years. C.T. pictured for himself a famous and comfortable future. What he did not account for was a serious illness.

Chapter 4

The Cambridge Seven

I'm afraid there is not much more we can do for him except make him comfortable. I don't expect him to recover from this illness," the doctor said as he snapped shut his bag. Then, in a softer tone, he turned to Mrs. Studd. "He is a strong young man. We can only pray for a miracle."

C.T. turned his head away so as not to see his mother cry. The truth was, he felt like crying himself. How could George be dying? It did not seem possible—or fair—but his brother lay unconscious in his bed. The illness, a bad case of pneumonia, had come on suddenly, and the doctor said there was little he could do to save George.

Hour after hour C.T. sat at George's bedside. He recalled the great cricketing moments that he and his brother had shared, beating Australia on the Cambridge team and taking the trip to Australia to retrieve the ashes. *But what use are they to George now?* C.T. asked himself. *What is all that fame and flattery worth? What is the point of spending your life chasing fame and wealth, when in the end you die and have to answer to God for the way you have lived? It could just as easily be me lying there, and George wiping my brow. What would happen if I were to die now? Where would I go?*

Such questions haunted C.T. He realized that even though he had become a Christian six years before, his life had continued to revolve around cricket. And although he had met his goal and become the most famous cricket player in England, it now seemed a silly thing to have spent his life pursuing. *No,* C.T. decided as he watched George gurgle and gasp for breath, *cricket would not last, honor would not last, nothing in the world would last.*

On the third day of the vigil at his brother's bedside, C.T. watched in amazement as George opened his eyes and grunted. This was the beginning of George's long, slow journey back from the brink of death to life.

C.T. was so grateful to think that God had spared his brother's life that when he heard that Dwight Moody was back in London for another mission, he vowed to go and hear him as soon as he could get away.

One wet night in November 1883, C.T. slipped into the back of the Moody Mission. Even before

Dwight Moody stood to speak, tears welled in C.T.'s eyes. C.T. bowed his head quietly and asked God to forgive him for getting caught up in worldly things rather than working for things of eternal value.

By the end of the meeting, C.T. felt a fire in his soul. When he had prayed with Mr. Weatherby, he had been too ashamed to tell people what he had done. This time his heart was overflowing with excitement. He arranged to meet with fellow members of the English cricket team and challenged them to come along to the Moody Mission with him. Many of them went, including the team captain, Ivo Bligh, and C.T.'s good friend Alan Steel. Much to C.T.'s delight, both men became Christians at the meetings, and this inspired C.T. to invite still more people. Within a week there were several more converts, and everyone in the cricket world knew that C.T. Studd had a new set of priorities.

In June 1884 the Moody Mission came to an end, and C.T. wondered what to do next. He had plenty of money to last him until his twenty-sixth birthday, when he would inherit enough to live comfortably for the rest of his life. As a result he did not need to enter a business or profession, and more and more his thoughts turned toward the thousands of people dying every day without having ever heard the gospel. The best years of C.T.'s life lay ahead, and C.T. determined to spend them serving Christ, though he was not sure how.

One evening a friend gave C.T. a tract written by an atheist. In the tract the atheist explained what he would do if he really thought Christianity was true, as so many Englishmen claimed it was. C.T. started to read.

> Did I firmly believe, as millions say they do, that the knowledge and practice of religion in this life influences destiny in another, religion would mean to me everything. I would cast away earthly enjoyments as dross, earthly cares as follies, and earthly thoughts and feelings as vanity. Religion would be my first waking thought, and my last image before sleep sank me into unconsciousness. I would labor in its cause alone. I would take thought for the morrow of eternity alone. I would esteem one soul gained for heaven worth a life of suffering.... I would strive to look upon eternity alone, and on the immortal souls around me, soon to be everlastingly happy or everlastingly miserable. I would go forth to the world and preach to it in season and out of season, and my text would be, WHAT SHALL IT PROFIT A MAN IF HE GAIN THE WHOLE WORLD AND LOSE HIS OWN SOUL?

Although the tract had been written to shame Christians because of their lack of action, it had the opposite effect on C.T. It made him want to act! Until then he had thought about preaching and teaching in England, but suddenly he felt as if he should go overseas, though he did not know where.

On Saturday, November 1, 1884, Stanley Smith, a friend and prizewinning rower from Cambridge University, invited C.T. to a meeting at the China Inland Mission headquarters at Pryland Road in London. Stanley, along with Dixon Hoste and William Cassels, had been accepted as missionaries with the China Inland Mission and were due to leave for Shanghai before Christmas. C.T. knew both Dixon and William. Dixon was leaving behind a promising career in the army to become a missionary, and upon graduating from Cambridge, William had been converted and then became a minister in South Lambeth, one of London's poorest slum areas.

That night at the China Inland Mission headquarters, a missionary who was returning to China the next day spoke. His name was John McCarthy, and as C.T. listened to what he had to say, his heart pounded. John spoke of his adventures walking across China from Wuhan in the east to Burma in the west. He spoke of thousands of Chinese people perishing every day with no knowledge of Jesus Christ.

By the end of the meeting, C.T. felt called to go to China himself, but he decided not to tell anyone right away. He thought that other people might consider it an impulsive decision, and he had his widowed mother to be concerned about. Even though Christianity had turned his family upside down, C.T. did not think his mother would be happy to see him leave for China.

For the next two weeks, C.T. prayed harder than he had ever prayed before. At the end of that time, he was even more convinced that God was calling him to work in China. He announced the decision to his mother as gently as he could.

Just as C.T. suspected, his mother was horrified. C.T.'s uncle accused him of breaking his mother's heart with foolish nonsense, and other family members begged C.T. not to throw his life away. They even sent Christian workers to explain to him how much work there was to be done in England. Even Kinny tried to dissuade C.T. from going. The whole family was in an uproar, and C.T. hated to go downstairs, where someone would inevitably be sobbing or preparing to plead with him to change his mind.

One night it was all too much for C.T., especially when Kinny asked him if he was proud of himself for breaking his mother's heart. The last thing C.T. wanted was to upset his widowed mother and bring stress to his family.

"Let's pray together," C.T. suggested to Kinny. "I don't want to be pigheaded. I just want to do God's will."

The two brothers prayed together about the situation, though neither of their minds was changed.

That night C.T. lay awake for a long time praying that God would give him peace. As he prayed, he heard the words, "Ask of Me and I will give thee the heathen for thine inheritance, and the uttermost parts of the earth for thy possession." That was enough for C.T. He got up the next morning with the assurance that God was truly calling him to China. And as long as he was sure about that, everything else paled in comparison. He determined to live for eternity, no matter what it cost him in terms of family ties or public opinion.

Now that the decision was final, C.T. visited Hudson Taylor, the founder and director of the China Inland Mission. At fifty-two years of age, Hudson Taylor had become a legend in missionary circles. Despite having buried a wife and two children in China, he had toiled on, making frequent trips inland himself and setting up a mission whose goal was to see the inland cities and towns evangelized.

C.T. liked Hudson Taylor from the moment they met. Taylor was a direct man who liked to get straight down to business. He made no promises other than hardships and deprivation, but he spoke of the wonderful blessing of preaching to people who had never once heard the name of Jesus Christ or the story of salvation. When C.T. announced that he felt called to China, Taylor was delighted. As the two of them talked, Taylor told C.T. that he would like to use his fame to challenge other young men with the needs of China. As a result, Taylor decided to delay the departure of Stanley Smith, Dixon Hoste, and William Cassels for China so that the three of them could join C.T. on a farewell tour of universities in Great Britain.

Another member was soon added to the group. Montagu Beauchamp, the son of a baron, was a childhood friend of the Studd family. In fact, his sister and Kinny Studd had just announced their engagement. Montagu, or Monty, as everyone called him, was also a Cambridge graduate and felt challenged by C.T.'s decision to go to China. The Beauchamp family were supporters of the China Inland Mission, but until C.T. announced his plan to go to China, Monty had never given any thought to the idea of being a missionary. Now, he told C.T., the thought gripped his heart, and he signed up to go with the group to China.

C.T. was stunned to think that his decision to become a missionary was already having an effect on other people. And although he was nervous speaking in front of crowds and often mumbled when he spoke, he liked being part of a team of young men who would go to China together. C.T. also continued to pray that his mother and family would be able to accept his going.

Within days of the meeting with Taylor, C.T. found himself at the center of a whirlwind of activity. The China Inland Mission (CIM) arranged for C.T., Stanley, Dixon, William, and Montagu to travel to Cambridge for a series of meetings. The news that one of the most famous cricketers in England, and one of their own, was headed to China caused quite a stir on campus. Hundreds of past and present students came to hear C.T. give his reasons for coming to such a decision.

C.T. explained his choice as simply as possible. When he was finished speaking, he invited anyone who wished to give his life to Christ or to dedicate himself to missions to come forward. He did not expect many to come, simply because he felt it would be difficult for young men to do such a thing in front of their peers. But he was wrong. As soon as the invitation was given, a stampede headed for the platform. One of those who came forward was Arthur Polhill-Turner, one of C.T.'s oldest and closet friends. Arthur confessed that God had also called him, along with his brother Cecil, to China.

Arthur and Cecil visited Hudson Taylor, and within days seven young men were preparing to go to China. Since all of them except Dixon Hoste had graduated from Cambridge University, the press dubbed them the "Cambridge Seven" and followed their every move.

The group continued its farewell tour, going as far north as Edinburgh. Everywhere they went they caused a sensation. Thousands of people came to hear why seven of the most privileged young men in all England would "throw away" everything to become missionaries half a world away.

Whenever he could find the time, C.T. wrote to his mother about the extraordinary tour. In one letter he wrote, "We had a grand meeting. They say there had never been such a meeting there before. The hall was crammed. We had a huge after-meeting. It was as if a charge of dynamite exploded among them."

When he got to Liverpool, he took out his fountain pen and began writing another letter to his mother. "Splendid news," he began. "The fire is still burning and over sixty professed conversions on that one night. I cannot tell how very much the Lord has blessed us...what a different life from my former one; why, cricket and racquets and shooting are nothing to this overwhelming joy. Finding out so much about not only the needs of the heathen, but also of the poor in London and all great towns has increased my horror at the luxurious way I have been living; so many suits and clothes of all sorts, while thousands are starving and perishing of cold."

C.T. lifted his pen from the paper and thought for a moment about all the needs of the people he had met since starting the tour with the Cambridge Seven. Until then he had barely spoken to a member of the English working class, except to his servants. Now he was filled with compassion for the hopeless lives they led. He began writing again. "So all must be sold when I come home if it has not been so before. Mother dear, I do pray God to show you that it is such a privilege to give up a child to be used of God to saving poor sinners who have never even heard the name of Jesus. God bless you, dear darling mother, and I know He will do it, and turn your sorrow into joy."

By the end of January the tour was coming to a close, and the China Inland Mission arranged for three final meetings, one at Cambridge, one at Oxford, and one in London. At 7:30 PM on February 2, 1885, the Guild Hall at Cambridge was overflowing with twelve hundred people, some of whom stood in the orchestra pit and crowded into the gallery. One of C.T.'s old teachers, Professor Babington, introduced the program. Then one by one the seven young men rose to speak. It was just three days before they were due to set sail for China, and the crowd listened with rapt attention.

Stanley Smith spoke first. "The love of Christ constrains us," he began, "to go into the world. Unless we spread abroad the light, we will find in England that we cannot hold our own with the powers of darkness."

The crowd cheered loudly.

When it was C.T.'s turn to speak, he rose and walked to the podium. He looked out at the sea of faces and said, "I want to recommend you to my Master. I have had many pleasures in my time, and have tasted most of the delights this world can give: but I can tell you that these pleasures are as nothing compared with my present joy. I had formerly as much love for cricket as any man could have, but when the Lord Jesus came into my heart, I found that I had something infinitely better. My heart was no longer set on the game: I wanted to win souls to serve and please Him."

Hundreds of people came forward at the end of the meeting, as they did in Oxford the following night.

On Wednesday, February 4, the Cambridge Seven held their last meeting, in Exeter Hall in London. It was the biggest of all their meetings, and once again the men took turns speaking, telling how they had come to the decision to go to China and of their love for God. C.T. was the last to speak, and he summed up the evening with a challenge.

"Are you living for the day, or are you living for life eternal?" he asked. "Are you going to care for the opinion of men here, or for the opinion of God? The opinion of men won't avail us much when we get before the judgment throne. But the opinion of God will. Had we not, then, better take His word and implicitly obey it?"

Following the meeting, C.T. spent the night at his family's house in Hyde Park. Although it was only eight years since the three oldest boys had dined there with their father after hearing Dwight Moody speak at Drury Lane, it seemed an age ago to C.T., so much had happened in his life since then. What would his father think of him now? Would he approve of his son's setting out for China to share the gospel? C.T. hoped he would, and he hoped his mother would come to accept it soon too.

C.T. hardly slept that night. He tossed and turned in his bed. Memories and questions haunted him. It was one thing to talk about giving up everything for Christ, but how would he feel when he was alone in a strange land, cold and hungry and missing his family? Would he long for his old life back? He hoped not, but he could not properly answer the question. Only the passage of time could do that.

Chapter 5

China at Last

A huge cheer went up from the crowd at Victoria Station in London as the whistle blew and a puff of steam engulfed the bystanders.

On board, twenty-four-year-old C.T. Studd strained for one last look at his family. The last person he could pick out of the crowd was his sixteen-year-old sister, Dora, who was wearing a bright blue dress. Kinny, his new wife, and his mother-in-law, Lady Beauchamp, were on board the train. They were accompanying the Cambridge Seven to Dover and then across the English Channel to Calais, France, where the missionary recruits would board a ship bound for the Orient.

Once they reached Calais, the Cambridge Seven found their second-class cabins and gathered for a time of prayer and singing. The other passengers were shocked to find that the young men, sons of England's finest gentlemen, were traveling second-class. But C.T. did not care; in fact, he welcomed it, knowing that his circumstances would be a lot grimmer when he ventured into China's inland territories.

The ship stopped at Brindisi, Italy, and Alexandria, Egypt, before passing through the Suez Canal. Then it was on to Colombo, on the island of Ceylon, and from there, Penang, Malaysia; Singapore; and Hong Kong. Whenever the ship docked, the enthusiastic young missionaries went ashore and preached to any group they could get together at such short notice. Early in the voyage the captain of the vessel was converted after talking with C.T., and he invited the young men to hold daily services on the quarterdeck.

The six-week voyage to China passed quickly, and on March 18, 1885, the Cambridge Seven arrived in Shanghai, China. As they walked down the gangplank and onto the bustling dock, a middle-aged Chinese man waved to them.

"Welcome to China!" the man yelled in perfect English.

It was only when the man was standing right in front of them that C.T. recognized him. It was Hudson Taylor! C.T. knew that the China Inland Mission had a policy of dressing like the Chinese people, right down to the impossibly wide-sleeved gowns and pigtails, but it was still a shock to see an English gentleman looking so Chinese.

Taylor escorted the seven men through immigration and then to the CIM hostel in Shanghai. He explained to them that their first task was to begin learning the Chinese language and start growing their hair long so that in three months they could begin their missionary travels.

Since Shanghai was a treaty port, one of China's cities open to foreign trade and foreign residents, thousands of Europeans lived there. Taylor booked Temperance Hall, the largest hall in the city, in which to hold a meeting to introduce China Inland Mission's newest missionaries to the English-speaking residents.

Just as in the Cambridge Seven's meetings in England, many people were converted and challenged to spread the gospel after hearing the Cambridge Seven speak. But it was Chinese people that C.T. longed to reach, and he was eager to be out among them.

In the weeks ahead, language study progressed slowly. C.T. and the Polhill-Turner brothers struggled more than the others with their lessons. Everyone persevered, however, and they were soon ready to travel to their various mission stations.

It was also time to put on Chinese dress. C.T. roared with laughter when Monty and Stanley shaved off their mustaches. And when the men all had the front half of their heads shaved and the remainder of their hair braided into queues (long, Chinese pigtails), they looked quite the part—except that Monty, Stanley, and C.T. were a good foot taller than any Chinese man.

Shoes proved to be the biggest challenge. The first shoemaker declared that he had never been asked to take on such a "gigantic" task as making shoes for C.T's large feet, and he fled in terror. A second shoemaker was warned before he reached the mission house of the large job ahead of him, and he accepted the challenge only after negotiating to be paid a good sum of money for his efforts. Finally C.T. got his shoes, but word of their size traveled quickly around the city, and whenever he went outside, Chinese people pointed at the shoes and laughed.

Still, C.T. had more important things to think about. It was time for the Cambridge Seven to split into two groups and travel inland. Stanley, Dixon, and William were assigned to go north to Shanxi province, while the Polhill-Turners and C.T. would head westward to Hanchung. Monty would stay in Shanghai, as he was not well.

On April 4, 1885, C.T. and Cecil and Arthur Polhill-Turner set out. They traveled seven hundred miles up the Yangtze River by steamer. The trip took four days, and C.T. spent most of that time on deck staring at the amazing scenery. Small villages dotted the riverbank, and all sorts of boats darted about on the river. Some carried fishermen, others ferried people from one side of the river to the other, and still others carried cargoes of grain and rice downriver to the market in Shanghai.

The steamer went no farther than Hankow, where the three missionaries transferred their belongings to a junk that would take them eleven hundred miles up the Han River to Hanchung. As C.T. stowed his baggage, he looked around at his new "home" for the next three months. He had to bend over to get into the three cabins, which were only six feet wide and seven feet long. One cabin was for him and the Polhill-Turner brothers, while the other two were for the captain and their Chinese language instructor. It was going to be a tight squeeze.

It was the first time that the three missionaries had been out of contact with any other Europeans, and C.T. soon found that there was a lot to get used to. The men were constantly stared at and poked by curious river folk, many of whom C.T. guessed had never seen a white person before. At first he did not mind this, but after a few days it became tedious to be the center of attention yet unable to answer a single question. There was another problem—rats. The rats overran the boat, nibbling everything in sight and stealing the men's socks to make their nests. The three missionaries thought of setting traps for the rats but decided to ask God to rid them of the annoying creatures. Amazingly, they did not have any more difficulty with the rats.

This gave C.T. an idea. C.T. was having a lot of difficulty with something else—the Chinese language. Why not ask God to perform a miracle and make the three of them know Chinese without having to learn it? The more C.T. thought about it, the more the idea appealed to him. He suggested it to Cecil and Arthur, who also thought it was a great idea. After all, they pointed out, wasn't God a God of miracles?

As the junk sailed up the Han River, the three missionaries stopped their language study and began to pray earnestly that God would pop the Chinese language into their heads while they slept. Each morning C.T. would wake up expecting Chinese words to be running through his mind, but they never were. Still, he kept praying and believing.

The hot, cramped voyage continued until they reached Hanchung, where they disembarked and set off northward for Pingyang-fu to meet Hudson Taylor. This time they traveled on foot. Their Chinese language instructor went with them, even though they no longer took language lessons from him. Two porters also accompanied them to help carry their luggage.

The group had many miles to cover, and C.T.'s days soon fell into a pattern. C.T. awoke at 2:00 AM and read his Bible by candlelight until 3:30. Then he got up and packed his few belongings back into his bag so that they could all be on their way at 4:00 AM. Normally they would walk eight or ten miles before stopping at a roadside inn for a breakfast of rice and soup. After breakfast they continued walking until they took a lunch break. Then they walked until the sun went down, when they finally stopped for the night. Most days they covered thirty miles. Soon the miles became agonizing to C.T., whose shoes wore out, forcing him to walk barefoot. When he was a child, C.T.'s mother had never let him run around without shoes and socks on his feet. As a result his feet were soft and tender, and they soon became swollen and infected. Despite his throbbing feet, C.T. would not allow his condition to slow the others down. They had a date with Hudson Taylor, and nothing was going to stand in their way, not even his blistered, bleeding feet.

The group finally reached Pingyang-fu on November 3. It had been seven months since they set out from Shanghai, and when they arrived, the three Europeans were suntanned and fit.

Taylor was eagerly awaiting their arrival, and one of the first things he asked was how their language study was going. C.T. was embarrassed as he told him they had given up studying in favor of waiting for a miracle.

Taylor nodded thoughtfully and then said, "If I could put Chinese into your heads with one wave of my hand, I would not do it." He went on to explain how important the process of learning was. By submitting to a Chinese scholar and watching what he did and listening to what he said, they were not only learning the language but also gaining much wisdom and understanding about the culture of the people they wanted to reach with the gospel.

C.T. agreed that he had made a mistake, and once again he took up the arduous task of learning Chinese. His first assignment helped hurry him along.

Taylor asked C.T. to go on to the town of Chin-Wu to keep a China Inland Mission station open. C.T. was completely alone among the Chinese in Chin-Wu, and he had little choice but to learn how to communicate effectively with them.

On December 2, 1885, C.T. remembered that it was his twenty-fifth birthday, though he had no one in particular to celebrate it with. Christmas and New Year soon rolled by, and C.T. began to feel at home among the people of Chin-Wu. He worked hard at his Chinese studies, and soon he was reading the Bible in Chinese to his cook.

By July 1886, however, C.T. was eager for some contact with other Europeans, and he was delighted to learn that he had been invited to a missionary conference in Taiyuen, the provincial capital of Shanxi province. He especially looked forward to seeing Stanley, William, Dixon, and Monty again.

As it happened, William really needed C.T. He was critically sick with smallpox, and the Chinese servants were not properly tending to the "white devil" in their care. C.T. stepped in right away, and together with Monty, he insisted on assuming the nursing duties. C.T. and Monty took turns looking after William and attending the conference meetings, at which both Hudson Taylor and his oldest son, Herbert, spoke. Thankfully, William made a speedy recovery.

At the end of the conference, C.T. and Taylor were scheduled to travel together to Chungking in Szechwan province to visit the CIM missionaries working there. However, before they set out on the journey, news reached them that riots had broken out in Chungking and all foreigners had been expelled from the city. When he heard this, C.T. immediately volunteered to go to Chungking and reopen the mission station there. It was agreed that another missionary, John Phelps, would accompany him.

The journey to Chungking was treacherous. Because of the riots, no inn was willing to accommodate "foreign devils," and so on several occasions C.T. and John found themselves sleeping for the night with the pigs in pigsties. When they finally reached Chungking, the two missionaries had to sneak into the city under the cover of dark, because Chinese guards had been posted to keep all foreigners out.

Inside the city C.T. And John found that the only European left was the British consul, Mr. Bourne.

"How did you get in here?" a surprised Mr. Bourne asked when he laid eyes on C.T. and John. "All Europeans who were not killed in the riots were forced to evacuate the city. I was allowed to stay because I am the British consul."

"We sneaked in after dark," C.T. said with a grin. "We have come to reopen the mission station."

"I am afraid you can't stay here. No foreigners except me are permitted to stay in the city at present. I can issue you a passport to travel up or down the river in safety, but you must leave," Mr. Bourne said.

"But we cannot leave. God has brought us safely this far, and we believe that that is because He wants us here. We will not go," C.T. answered.

Mr. Bourne looked startled. "You are a very stubborn man, Mr. Studd. I have a small room here in my house, but it is big enough for only one man to live in. I will allow one of you to stay, but the other must leave." Then he studied both of them and announced, "Studd, you will stay with me."

C.T. moved into the room in Mr. Bourne's house. After he had seen John Phelps off, he set about locating the local Chinese Christians, setting up meetings to encourage them in their faith.

Time in Chungking passed quickly for C.T. He was surprised when one morning he received a thick letter in the mail. The letter bore the watermark of Messrs. Coutts & Co, the Studd family's solicitor. As C.T. tore the envelope open, he realized that it had been two weeks since his twenty-sixth birthday, the day he was to inherit the money his father had left him. Sure enough, the envelope contained copies of stocks and bank deposits that now belonged to him.

When he added it all up, C.T. calculated that he had been left at least twenty-nine thousand pounds, enough money to live comfortably for the rest of his life. But that was not what he had in mind for the money. For two years now, he had been sure of what he wanted to do when he received the inheritance—he wanted to give the money to Christian charities. He thanked God that he was in Chungking, because he needed a British official to sign the papers giving his brother Kinny the necessary authority to dispose of the money.

Later that day C.T. found Mr. Bourne in his study.

"May I come in?" he asked.

"By all means, my good man. What can I help you with?" Mr. Bourne asked.

C.T. got straight to the point. "I received mail this morning. It was information about my inheritance, which I had almost forgotten about. Would you be able to draw up and sign some papers so that my brother can have power of attorney over the money? I wish him to give it away on my behalf."

C.T. watched as Mr. Bourne's face turned white. Mr. Bourne caught his breath and then spluttered, "But...but it would be quite a sum of money, wouldn't it? I mean, your father was a wealthy man."

"He was," C.T. agreed, "but he found the Lord just two years before he died, and I am sure he would approve of my giving it away. More important, I know my heavenly Father approves. There is no safer place for my money than in 'God's bank.' He offers one-hundredfold increase. Do you know anyone who offers better interest than that?"

"You...I...no!" the consul replied. "I won't let you do it. You need to think about this in the cold light of day." Then he softened his tone. "You will always need food and a roof over your head, and you might marry one day and have children. Think ahead a little. After all, you may like being a missionary now, but ten years from now, who can tell?"

C.T. was shocked. He never imagined that he would have to fight with his host to get him to sign the papers.

"But it's your duty to sign them," he said. "I am a British subject, and you are the resident consul."

Mr. Bourne threw up his hands and sighed. "Very well, but I am going to insist on this: take two weeks to think it over, and if you haven't changed your mind—and I am sure that when you think seriously about it, you will—then I will sign the documents for you."

C.T. went away satisfied that he had to wait only two weeks before he could carry out his plan.

In the following days C.T. settled on how the money should be divided up. He decided on four allotments of five thousand pounds each. The first allotment was for Dwight L. Moody, the man who had converted his father. C.T. wanted Moody to use the money to start a gospel work in Tirhoot, North India, where his father had made his fortune producing indigo dye.

The second allotment was for George Müller, a Prussian man who had emigrated to England and now ran Christian orphanages for the poorest children in Bristol.

C.T. chose George Holland to receive the third allotment. Holland was a zealous preacher who worked with the poor in Whitechapel, London.

The fourth allotment was to go to Commissioner Frederick Booth-Tucker, General William Booth's son-in-law, who had advanced the Salvation Army into India.

C.T. divided the rest of the money up among other missions and Christian charities he admired.

Two weeks later C.T. was back in Mr. Bourne's office, asking him to draw up the papers. Although the consul was not happy about it, he agreed that C.T. had waited the agreed-upon two weeks.

On January 13, 1887, C.T. sent off the paperwork, glad that his money was now safely deposited in the "Bank of Heaven," as he called it.

Within a month some of the veteran missionaries who had worked in Chungking before the riots began to trickle back into town, and C.T. decided that it was time to head back to Shanghai. He had heard that his brother George would be traveling through the port sometime in spring, and he was anxious to see him again. He did not know that this trip would change the course of his life.

Chapter 6

He Had Never Met a Woman Like Priscilla

In April 1887 C.T. arrived back in Shanghai. The trip had been long and arduous, but he enjoyed every moment of it. By now he had come to savor rice three times a day and had gotten used to the hard, brick beds in the local inns. He marveled that he now felt as much at home in China as he had in England.

Three other English people were staying at the CIM guest house in Shanghai, and C.T. enjoyed their company. The three were Miss Black, an elderly spinster who was the hostess of the guest house; Mr. Stevenson, the deputy director of CIM who was passing through Shanghai; and Priscilla Stewart, a young Irish woman who had recently arrived and was too ill with heart problems to travel inland.

Several letters were waiting for C.T. in Shanghai. One was from Dwight L. Moody, thanking C.T. for his generous gift and explaining that he was not ready to start a work in India yet. Instead he hoped that C.T. would approve of the money going toward starting the Moody Bible Institute in Chicago, where young men and women would be trained as missionaries and sent around the world. C.T. was satisfied with this outcome. Another letter was from Frederick Booth-Tucker in India. Booth-Tucker informed C.T. that his gift had enabled General Booth to send fifty Salvation Army officers from England to the subcontinent of India. These new officers were causing quite a stir there, and many lower-caste Indians were responding to the gospel.

C.T. asked Mr. Stevenson if he could read an excerpt from Booth-Tucker's letter at devotions the following morning. On his way to devotions the next morning, he bounded down the stairs two at a time. As he turned to walk into the front room, he caught a glimpse of Priscilla Stewart at the top of the stairs. Priscilla looked frail and sickly as she edged her way along the banister. C.T. could not bear to watch her descend the stairs, so he hurried in to join the others in the front room.

"That woman has made a real mistake in coming to China!" C.T. exclaimed to Mr. Stevenson. "It seems as if the life has been sucked from her, and I'm sure that she could never stand the rigors of the interior."

"You could be right," Mr. Stevenson agreed. "Even the smallest task seems to take a great amount of effort for her."

Priscilla walked into the room, and C.T. fished around in his pocket for the letter. The small group sang a couple of hymns, and then Mr. Stevenson asked C.T. to read the letter. The letter began with thanks for C.T.'s donation and then went on to say,

> We opened at Kandy, the capital of Ceylon, on Christmas Eve. It has a population of about 30,000. We sent a simple Scottish lass and a rough native servant girl. The former is quite uneducated. Her orthography is—well, peculiar. She has been slow to learn the language, and after three months' hard work could only speak a few sentences, giving her testimony, leading the meetings, etc. Her lieutenant knew no English. Yet the two went bravely and took charge of a hall to hold about 250.... The result—in the course of about two months they had at least 100 souls and were able to enroll about fifty regular soldiers, several of whom have already been taken into the work as officers. Never before have native women been known to speak in public, but now there is a good band of them testifying nightly on the platform.

C.T. stopped reading for a moment, and Priscilla Stewart spoke.

"How wonderful what the Lord is able to do with even the most humble of His servants!" she exclaimed.

Priscilla's eyes glowed as she spoke, and C.T. felt ashamed of what he had said to Mr. Stevenson. Perhaps, he chastised himself, his judgement of this young woman had been too hasty.

Later that day, C.T. and Priscilla found themselves alone on the veranda of the guest house, and Priscilla began to tell C.T. why she had come to China.

"It began," she said forthrightly, "when two of my uncles were converted and became extremely active in the Lord's work. The rest of the family, including me, was embarrassed by this turn of events. After all, we were a prominent family in Belfast—good Anglicans, but not the type of people who felt it good manners to delve into the personal matter of another person's soul."

As she stopped to take a sip of tea, C.T. marveled at the similarity of their upbringings. They were both rich and privileged and leading good lives until someone in the family was converted.

Priscilla's voice broke into C.T.'s thoughts. "I was happy just the way I was, especially when I was allowed to start going to balls at eighteen. I had a wonderful time at my first one, but that night I had a terrifying dream. In it Jesus came to me and He did not recognize me. Instead he said, 'Depart from Me. I never knew you.' I tried everything I could to get those words out of my mind, but as the years went by they would not go away.

"Then, when I was twenty-two, I went to stay with a friend of my mother. It turned out that she had been recently converted, and she and her father took me along to a Salvation Army meeting. Oh, I will never forget how uncomfortable I felt that night. I sat on the platform with my hostess, with hundreds of Salvation Army lassies all around me. Their stiff collars and studs creaked as they moved, and they took their tambourines and flapped them around my head! I was in a state, but I got away, and thankfully no one asked about my soul.

"When I arrived home, my hostess drew my attention to a pamphlet written by General Booth describing a terrible vision he had had of a lot of people shipwrecked. You could see the people with their heads above the water and their hands stretching out, and some of them on the rocks. Someone was telling how Jesus would return suddenly, and then the same awful state was going to overtake the unsaved.

"Suddenly I realized that I had been very wrong. I would have given anything to get to God, but I could not. My heart was as black as the worst sinner's on earth. I was so convicted of unbelief, mocking, and scoffing, that I was the most hell-deserving sinner that ever lived. I fell to my knees and waited. I saw a vision of Jesus on the cross. When it finally faded, I realized that I had been on my knees for two hours. My hostess said, 'What have you seen?' and I replied, 'I have seen Calvary, and forever Jesus will be my Lord and my God.'"

"So you joined the Salvation Army after that?" C.T. asked.

"Yes. I found their meetings a great joy. Those were such grand days. I would march with them, and people would throw rotten eggs, stones, and even old boots at us, but I didn't care. I was marching for Jesus. Then God called me to China to work with CIM, and I obeyed His command."

The pair sat in silence for a while. C.T. was too astonished to speak. He had expected Priscilla Stewart to be as timid as her walking steps, but when she spoke, her words burned into his soul. C.T. knew that he wanted to spend more time with this amazing young woman, and he was glad it was still two weeks before George was expected in Shanghai.

Although C.T. spoke reasonable Chinese, he spoke a western dialect and had a hard time making himself understood in Shanghai. Instead of preaching to the Chinese, he filled in the time running evangelistic meetings for English sailors. As soon as Priscilla heard what C.T. was doing, she insisted on joining him. C.T. led the meetings, but it was Priscilla's fiery testimony that brought about the conversion of a number of burly sailors. As C.T. watched Priscilla speak, her eyes flashed with an intensity he found irresistible. He had to admit to himself that he had never before met a woman like Priscilla Stewart.

In due course George Studd arrived in Shanghai, and he and C.T. had a wonderful reunion. George brought news of the family. Kinny was the proud father of a new son, and their sister, Dora, had recently married Willie Bradshaw, a family friend.

Eventually Priscilla's health improved, and she was cleared to begin the journey to the inland mission station she had been assigned to. C.T. was sorry to see her leave, but soon afterward he set off for northern China to preach in small towns and villages. George, who had not come to be a missionary himself, went along with C.T. as his unofficial assistant. C.T. was glad for the company, but even so, he found his thoughts often turned to Priscilla. Finally he decided he had to do something about the situation. After praying and fasting for eight days, he made a decision: he would ask Priscilla to marry him.

The following day, July 25, C.T. wrote Priscilla a letter. He got straight to the point, asking her to be his bride. Then he outlined the kind of life they would lead together:

> It will be no easy life, no life of ease which I could offer you, but one of toil and hardship; in fact, if I did not know you to be a woman of God, I would not dream of asking you. It is to be a fellow soldier in His Army. It is to live a life of faith in God, a fighting life, remembering that here we have no abiding city, no certain dwelling place, but only a home eternal in the Father's House above. Such would be the life: may the Lord alone guide you.

Priscilla's reply was less than C.T. had hoped for. She was not convinced that God wanted her to marry him. She said, however, that she would keep praying about C.T.'s proposal. C.T. fired off another letter to her, and another, until in October he finally got the answer he had prayed for. Priscilla agreed to be his wife.

C.T. was overjoyed. He sat down right away to write to his mother. It was only then that he realized how little practical information he had about his future wife. He did not know her age, how much schooling she'd had, her parents' names, or how many brothers and sisters she had. But this did not daunt C.T. He knew Priscilla's commitment to God, and that was what mattered most to him.

C.T. expressed this feeling in his next letter to Priscilla, dated October 14, 1887.

> I laugh when I think of how little I know of you my own darling, not even your age or anything, only it's more than enough for me that you are a true child and lover of the Lord Jesus, that He has knit my heart to yours and yours to mine to work together for Him with all our hearts and souls and minds till He come.... I love you for your love to Jesus, I love you for your zeal toward Him, I love you for your faith in Him, I love you for your love of souls, I love you for loving me, I love you for your own self, I love you for ever and ever. I love you because Jesus has

used you to bless me and fire my soul. I love you because you will always be a red-hot poker making me run faster. Lord Jesus, how can I ever thank You enough for such a gift?

The two of them did not know when they would see each other again, as they were both busy with their missionary work, but December 26, 1887, changed everything. That day C.T. received a letter from one of Priscilla's coworkers. The letter contained bad news. Priscilla was gravely ill with pneumonia. C.T.'s mind went back to the time when he had first met her. Priscilla was extremely weak from heart problems, and he wondered whether the pneumonia might be fatal in her weakened condition. He did not know, and he was unwilling to wait around and find out. He calculated that if he traveled day and night, he could be at Priscilla's station in Hoh-chau in three days. He set out immediately, praying all the way that she would recover her strength.

Thankfully his prayers were answered. C.T. arrived at the mission station to find that Priscilla was over the worst of her illness. She was delighted to see him, and the two of them spent many hours praying and reading together. C.T. was also impressed with the work Priscilla and three other single women had accomplished. It had not been easy for them in Hoh-chau, but slowly they had found ways to share the gospel with the residents of the town. Recently they had seen their first converts, and the nucleus of a small church was forming.

Stanley Smith arrived in Hoh-chau several days later, and he and C.T. decided to journey back to northern China together. It was difficult for C.T. to part with Priscilla again, but they both felt that the time was not yet right for them to marry.

Stanley and C.T. had reached Hungtung when it became evident that they would not be going any farther for a while. Stanley had typhoid fever, and C.T. set about nursing him.

It was three weeks before Stanley was well enough to travel, and in that time C.T. had had plenty of time to think about his future. He believed that God wanted him and Priscilla to be married, and he could no longer think of any reason to wait. Instead of continuing northward, C.T. and Stanley headed back to Hoh-chau.

Priscilla was both surprised and delighted to see the two men again so soon, and she agreed that it was time for a wedding. She packed up her bags and prepared to accompany C.T. to Tientsin, where the nearest British consul resided.

The couple's decision to do this caused shock waves among the new converts of Hoh-chau. In the town, unmarried men and women were not permitted to see each other's face, and here were two unmarried missionaries planning to travel across the country together. The converts told C.T. that it was unthinkable to do such a thing, and so C.T. and Priscilla agreed to have a Chinese wedding before they left Hoh-chau.

Arrangements were quickly made, and a visiting Chinese evangelist, Pastor Shi, offered to officiate at the service. Priscilla and C.T. dressed in their usual Chinese attire, though Priscilla added a white sash with the words "United to fight for Jesus" written across it. C.T. smiled when he saw the sash. He had certainly found himself a fiery woman for his wife.

After the ceremony everyone was invited to a feast at the mission house, and the next day C.T. and Priscilla set out for Tientsin. Along the way C.T. managed to learn some more about his companion. Priscilla was born on August 28, 1864, making her four years younger than he was. She got her golden-colored hair from her father and her petite build from her mother.

C.T. wondered out loud what they would do for a wedding ring, and Priscilla produced the answer from her baggage. Before she left Ireland, she explained, a close friend had presented her with a ring as a memento. Priscilla showed the ring to C.T. Amazingly, when it had been given to her in Ireland, it had the initials C.T.S. engraved on the inside! C.T. took this as an added sign that God had approved their marriage.

When they reached Tientsin, a letter was waiting for C.T. It was from his solicitor in England, explaining that all of the money had been dispersed according to C.T.'s instructions. However, a surplus of three thousand four hundred pounds was still left, and the solicitor wanted to know what to do with it. Since he was now married and this was the last money he had, C.T. decided to give it to Priscilla and let her decide what to do with it. She shook her head when he presented the money to her.

"C.T.," she said, "what did the Lord tell the rich young man to do?"

"Sell all," C.T. replied.

"Well then, we will start clear with the Lord at our wedding. Give the money to the Salvation Army and let us trust God together for our needs," Priscilla said cheerfully and firmly.

Once again C.T. was impressed with the dedication of the young Irish woman who had consented to be his bride.

The second wedding, in Tientsin, was a small affair and took place on a beautiful spring morning on April 7, 1888. Most of the missionaries present at the service were horrified that the couple did not wear specially made Western wedding clothes. C.T. and Priscilla had decided against this. They could not see the point of wasting money on such clothes.

At the end of the service, C.T. and Priscilla knelt side by side and made a promise to God and to each other: "We will never hinder one another from serving Thee."

In the years ahead, fulfilling that promise would cost them more than anyone present at the wedding could have ever imagined.

Chapter 7

Foreign Devils

Leave now, you white devils! You will bring bad luck to all of us!" an old Chinese man yelled as C.T., Priscilla, and their coworker Mary Burroughs stood in the marketplace of Lungang-Fu.

C.T. waited for the tirade to end. He did not blame the man or the others who were encouraging him on. After all, the missionary trio were probably the first white people they had ever seen. C.T. also was aware that the people of inland China knew little about the outside world. They had been taught that China was in the shape of a huge circle that touched the edges of a square. The corners of the square, which fell outside the circle, contained the rest of the world, the "Kingdom of the Foreign Devils." The people had no idea that different countries or religions existed beyond their own.

After about half an hour, the crowd that had gathered about the missionaries dispersed, and C.T. was able to ask a millet vendor if he knew of any houses in the city that were for rent. At first the man told C.T. that every house was taken, but when C.T. was not satisfied with the man's answer, the man said that there was one empty house, and for good reason—it was said to be haunted.

As C.T., Priscilla, and Mary trudged up the cobblestone street in the direction the millet vendor had pointed, people hurried past them, cursing or spitting at the foreign devils. Near the top of the street, the three missionaries found an abandoned house. C.T. pushed open the creaking gate, and the trio stepped into the overgrown courtyard. The door to the house flapped on its hinges. C.T., Priscilla, and Mary went inside. The whitewashed walls were faded and bare, and scorpions scuttled across the uneven, brick floor. A brick platform bed sat against the far wall, and a fireplace was in the center of the room. Another room had a brick bed and a small stool in it and a tiny window without a windowpane. A third room was empty, and C.T. thought it would make a fine kitchen and dining room. The house was hardly luxurious, but it would provide a roof over their heads and an inroad into the town, which had never heard the gospel. A smaller building, which C.T. imagined using as a chapel, was on the other side of the courtyard.

C.T. escorted the two women back to the market, where their porters and donkeys were waiting.

Together they all set off to find the man who owned the house. When C.T. found the owner, he was able to convince him to rent the house to the missionaries, though he was sure that the owner made them pay more for it than it was worth.

It did not take long for the three missionaries to settle in. All they had brought with them was an extra set of Chinese clothing each, some pots and plates, and a few personal items, such as combs and mirrors. These few items became an irresistible draw to the neighbors, who peered in the window and the open doorway to see what the "white devils" were up to. C.T., Priscilla, and Mary made a point of looking welcoming, even though they would rather have shut the door on the prying eyes and enjoyed some privacy.

Not all the neighbors were inquisitive or tolerant of the missionaries. Whenever the missionaries ventured out of the house, they were subjected to volleys of cursing and spitting. It was worse when C.T. and Priscilla went out together, because they walked side by side down the road. Chinese custom dictated that a wife should walk three steps behind her husband, but C.T. and Priscilla felt that it was important for people to see that in a Christian marriage men and women were equal. This led to a lot of mocking and mimicking, but C.T. and Priscilla did not mind. The people were at least taking note of the point they were trying to make.

There was one bright spot during the first few months at their new post in Lungang-Fu. Priscilla announced that she was expecting a baby. The child was due in February 1889. The question C.T. and Priscilla now began asking themselves was, should they leave their post and travel to a China Inland Mission hospital to have the baby? C.T. calculated that they would need to leave Lungang-Fu three months before the baby was due and stay away for two months after the child was born, when Priscilla would be strong enough to travel again. Although C.T. could not justify being away from his mission station for that length of time, he left the final decision to his wife. Priscilla decided that they should stay in Lungang-Fu and trust God to keep them safe.

As it turned out, C.T. soon had cause to wonder just how safe they would be staying at the mission station to have their baby. The mandarin, whose word was law in Lungang-Fu, did not like having English people in his city, and he constantly stirred up opposition to the missionaries and refused to allow C.T. to preach in the streets. Also, as the first year dragged on, a drought set in. The crops in the region around Lungang-Fu failed, and the land was soon parched. The people of the town were quick to blame the foreign devils for the drought, saying that their gods were angry that Christians were living among them.

Then in September, C.T. noticed a placard in the marketplace. His blood chilled as he read it. The placard announced that the following day everyone in the town was to shut the door to his courtyard and place burning incense outside it as a sign of worship to the rain god. He also overheard two men saying that a group of men were about to set out to get the rain god from a nearby town. The rain god would be paraded through the streets of Lungang-Fu so that he could smell all the incense offered to him. C.T. hurried home to tell Priscilla and Mary what he had read and overheard.

"What will we do?" Priscilla asked. "You know they will be very insulted when we do not burn incense, and they will blame us for angering their god even more."

"I think it is one of the mandarin's schemes. He has been looking for a way to get rid of us ever since we arrived, and what better way than to have people rioting outside our house," Mary said.

C.T. sighed. What could they do?

That night C.T. and Priscilla stayed up late praying about the situation. When they awoke the following morning, the air was filled with the sweet smell of incense. C.T. locked the doors and waited to see what would happen next.

About midday they heard the procession at the top of the street. As it got closer, they could hear the chanting. "We want rain. We want rain. Kill the foreign devils. Kill the foreign devils!"

Crash! C.T. heard a thud against the back wall of the chapel, and then he smelled the choking odor of acrid smoke. The mob had set fire to the building. C.T. acted quickly. He scooped up Priscilla and carried her out into the courtyard.

"Look after her," he yelled to Mary as he climbed over the sidewall and ran off in the direction of the mandarin's hall. It was a mandarin's duty to help those who came to him for protection.

C.T. sprinted all the way to the mandarin's hall, only to find that the mandarin was not there. In fact, the mandarin was not anywhere in the city. He had conveniently left town when he heard about the parade with the rain god. *No doubt,* C.T. mused, *so that he won't have the blood of foreigners on his hands.*

Since he could not plead with the mandarin to intervene, C.T. could do nothing but go back to the house and try to help the women. As he ran back up the street, no one paid him much attention. All eyes were fixed on the men who had set the chapel alight. The men had now turned their attention to the outer wall of the mission house and were attacking it with picks and axes.

C.T. stood for a moment, wondering how he was going to get back inside the mission compound, when he heard a voice raised above the crowd. It belonged to a scholar C.T. had enjoyed several conversations with.

"What are you doing?" the scholar yelled at the mob. "While you are wasting time, the day is passing. Look at the rain god—he is sitting in shadows. Pick him up quickly and take him into the sunlight. He needs the sunlight in order to bless us with rain."

In an instant the shouting stopped, and the people turned to look at the rain god, a stone statue about three feet high that had been set down in a doorway.

"If you neglect him, he will neglect you," the scholar continued, and that idea seemed to galvanize the mob into action. Above all, they did not want to anger the rain god.

The men quickly dropped the axes and picks they were wielding against the wall of the house, and with a cheer, six men picked up the stone statue and heaved it up onto their shoulders. The men set off marching toward the market, and everyone followed behind them.

C.T. stood with his head bowed, waiting for the mob to pass and thanking God for saving the three of them from death.

By now the south wall of the chapel was a smoldering heap of rubble, but Priscilla and Mary were unhurt, and the mission house itself had not been touched on the inside.

The mob did not return that day, and even though rain did not come for another six months, the missionaries were not bothered again.

Much to C.T.'s surprise, after the incident local people began to seek him out to talk to him about religion. As a result of talking to C.T., many of these people became interested in Christianity.

One of the first men to become a Christian was a visitor to Lungang-Fu. His name was Liu, and at first he doubted whether the Christian God would want to have anything to do with him.

"I am a murderer," he confessed to C.T., "and an adulterer and an opium addict. I've broken all the rules of God and man again and again."

C.T. assured Liu that God would forgive him if he repented of the things he had done. Liu did so and was converted. Soon afterward he told C.T., "I must go back home to the town where I have committed such evil sins and tell the people the glad tidings of Jesus' love."

After Liu left, C.T. prayed for him every day.

Two months later, in February 1889, Liu returned to the mission house in Lungang-Fu with a story to tell.

"As soon as I arrived home," Liu began, "I started to tell my father and my brothers about the God who had changed my life from the inside out. They did not want to hear about this because it reminded them of their own wicked hearts. They took me to the mandarin, who ordered me to be beaten with two thousand lashes with a bamboo cane. I prayed as each lash fell on my back until I became unconscious." Liu paused to pull up the back of his shirt. His back was crisscrossed with fresh scars.

"Praise be to God," Liu went on. "I woke up in a Christian hospital. I learned that some of my friends had put me on an oxcart and taken me there. Of course, my first thoughts were that I must go back and keep preaching in my town, but my friends tried to restrain me. They said that the mandarin would have me killed the next time I showed my face there. But I was sure that God wanted me to go back there."

A big smile spread over Liu's face.

"So I climbed out an open hospital window in the night and returned to my hometown," Liu continued. "In the morning I started telling people about Jesus. Sure enough, I was brought before the mandarin again, and this time he had me thrown in prison. What a wonderful place prison is!" Liu grinned. "I had all day to witness to the other prisoners through a hole in my door. Eventually the jailer released me, saying that I was causing too much confusion among the prisoners and the guards. God is good, is He not?"

"Yes, God is good," C.T. agreed, amazed at the man's simple faith and the price he had cheerfully paid for it. Listening to Liu made all of the cursing and spitting the missionaries had endured worth it.

Later that month Priscilla gave birth to a baby girl. C.T. delivered the baby, whom they named Grace. Their Chinese cook lingered around the baby until C.T. asked her why she spent so much time staring at the child.

"I was wondering if you intended to keep it, since it is a girl," the cook said.

"What do you mean?" C.T. asked.

The cook shrugged her shoulders. "Many mothers do not keep their girls, especially if they don't have a boy already. There are certain pagodas outside the city where a mother can leave a baby girl. The wolves make quick work of them."

C.T.'s stomach turned. Although he did not doubt what he heard, he was still appalled at the thought that a parent could take an innocent baby and leave it for wild animals to devour. He looked down at Grace and shook his head.

"The Christian God tells us to value all life," he explained patiently. "In His kingdom we are all one. Boys are no better than girls."

Sadly, Priscilla had fallen gravely ill after Grace was born. C.T. was relieved when a CIM nurse named Jessie Kerr came to visit them in Lungang-Fu, especially since Mary Burroughs was no longer working at the station.

After spending a few hours with Priscilla, Jessie had grim news for C.T. "Mr. Studd," she said, "I've tried every mortal thing that I can think of, but nothing seems to have any effect. Mrs. Studd is growing rapidly worse. I hate to say this, but I cannot give you any hope that she will recover. If by some miracle God does spare her life, you must take her home to England at once."

As the words sunk into his head, something within C.T. rose up. Take his wife home? After God had called them to China! C.T. gathered a small band of Chinese Christians around Priscilla's bed, and they anointed her with oil and prayed that God would heal her. C.T. prayed through the night, and by the following morning, Priscilla was well on the way to recovery. C.T. and the small band of Christians then held a thanksgiving service, and it was not long before Priscilla was up and about and able to get on with her missionary work as well as take care of Grace.

In the spring Stanley Smith, one of the Cambridge Seven, and his new wife joined the Studds at the mission station in Lungang-Fu. The four of them decided to set up an opium refuge for opium addicts. At first only a few homeless men dared seek help from Christians. However, as a result of prayer and dedicated nursing, some of the men were set free from their addiction, and other addicts began to come to the refuge.

Pastor Shi, who had officiated at C.T. and Priscilla's Chinese wedding ceremony in Hoh-chau, joined the missionaries in Lungang-Fu, and the work began to flourish. Several large personal donations from friends in England allowed C.T. to buy a larger house so that the opium refuge could be expanded.

When Grace was one year old, Priscilla gave birth to another child. This time it was a boy, whom they named Paul. Sadly, Paul lived for only a few hours. C.T. buried him in the corner of the courtyard. He marveled that Priscilla never shed a tear in front of him. Instead Priscilla redoubled her efforts to reach the women of the community with the gospel.

Other obstacles occurred along the way. Since C.T. had given all his inheritance away, he and Priscilla had no regular means of support. Friends or churches in England would send them money from time to time, and because C.T. and Priscilla's lifestyle was very simple, the couple normally had enough money to cover their expenses. However, one day soon after Paul died, they had no money and no food in the house. C.T. and Priscilla agreed to pray through the night about their situation.

After about twenty minutes on their knees, C.T. announced that they had prayed long enough. "We have told God everything," he said, "and there seems no point in repeating it, as if He were deaf or could not understand the urgency of the situation."

The following morning the twice-monthly mailbag arrived. C.T. and Priscilla quickly began to open the letters in the bag, hoping to find a check from someone they knew. But there were no checks in any of the letters. C.T. decided to check inside the mailbag one more time. This time he spotted a single letter that had gotten stuck in the corner of the bag. He pulled the letter out and studied the unfamiliar handwriting on the envelope.

"Do you know a Mr. Frank Crossley?" C.T. asked his wife.

"No," she replied. "I don't recall ever hearing that name before."

C.T. slit the envelope open and unfolded a letter. Inside was a check for one hundred pounds. The letter also contained an explanation: "I have for some reason or another received a command of God to send you a check for one hundred pounds. I've never met you, I've only heard of you, and that not often, but God's prevented me from sleeping tonight by His command. Why He should command me to send you this I do not know—you will know better than I. Anyhow, here it is, and I hope it will do you good."

C.T. and Priscilla held a prayer meeting to thank God right there and then.

The mission work in Lungang-Fu continued on, and by 1894 the opium refuge was housing fifty people at a time, mostly men but also some women and even a few children.

By now the number of children in the Studd household had increased by three. Dorothy, Edith, and Pauline all were born about a year apart. Having given birth to five babies in less than six years had physically worn out Priscilla, and C.T.'s health was not much better. C.T. had developed asthma from the harsh climate and the smoke-filled rooms he spent so much of his time in while sharing the gospel with people.

A letter soon arrived from C.T.'s mother, asking him to come home to England for a break. She had heard from other missionaries about C.T.'s and Priscilla's dire physical conditions and enclosed enough money to cover all their travel expenses for the journey home. C.T. was not sure, however, that they should all go back to England for a break. He prayed about the matter for six months before he felt it was the right thing to do. But once C.T. was convinced it was the right thing to do, the family quickly packed up and headed east for Shanghai.

C.T. had left England ten years before as a fit and agile sports hero and a single man. Now he was returning in ill health and with a wife and four little girls, none of whom spoke any English! As they boarded the steamer for England in Shanghai, C.T. wondered how they would ever adjust to the ways of his upper-class family. And for that matter, how would he fit back into "fashionable" society?

Chapter 8

India

Daddy, Daddy!" C.T. looked up to see his three oldest daughters, led by six-year-old Grace, enter the cabin. They all had shocked looks on their faces.

"What is it, girls?" he asked.

"We don't understand those missionaries at all," Grace said emphatically. "They only play music, and they never sing hymns or pray! What is wrong with them?"

C.T. thought for a moment and then roared with laughter. The "missionaries" his daughters could not figure out were in fact members of a brass band traveling on the ship with them. The band held a concert every afternoon, and the girls were allowed to sit and listen. But none of C.T.'s daughters had ever seen a white person before who wasn't a missionary.

Eventually, after the children had been holed up in their cramped quarters for too long, the ship docked in London. Kinny, whom C.T. had not seen for ten years, was waiting to meet them.

After they had disembarked, C.T. sent Priscilla and the four girls on ahead to his mother's house at Hyde Park Gardens while he waited with Kinny for their luggage to be off-loaded.

As the two brothers waited, they had much to talk about. While C.T. had been in China, Kinny had made a successful evangelistic trip to the United States at the invitation of Dwight L. Moody. He told C.T. how many American universities had opened their halls to him so that he could tell the students about the Cambridge Seven. Many of these students caught the vision for missionary service after listening to Kinny, and they began a group called the Student Christian Movement. The Student Christian Movement's goal was to mobilize thousands of American students to take the gospel to the ends of the earth, with the hope of evangelizing the entire world in a single generation.

C.T. listened eagerly to Kinny. He wished he were well enough to start a similar tour of his own to tell people about the need for missionaries in China. But his health would not allow it. His chest hurt so much that C.T. wondered whether he had tuberculosis rather than asthma.

After the family had settled into the Hyde Park Gardens home, C.T.'s mother insisted that he and

Priscilla and the children have a medical checkup. During the checkup the doctor confirmed that C.T. had developed chronic asthma and not tuberculosis. The doctor also discovered that Priscilla's heart condition had worsened after giving birth to five children and that Priscilla was again pregnant. The girls, though, were thriving.

At the Hyde Park Gardens home, the girls were a source of both frustration and amusement to their parents. C.T.'s mother ran the house according to a firm routine. She had a cook, a butler, and two housemaids to service her needs and the needs of her guests. And when she heard that C.T. was coming home, she hired a nursemaid for Pauline and a nanny for the other three girls. And that is where the trouble began. The children spoke little English, and the nanny had difficulty communicating with them. Many of the things she tried to get them to do made no sense to the girls' Chinese way of thinking. And when the children became too much for her, she would lock one of them in the bathroom. When she did this, the other girls would gang together and dance around the nanny, chanting loudly in Chinese. The frightened nanny would then have to release the "captive" for the sake of peace.

Gradually the girls began to settle, and Priscilla prepared for the birth of another baby. For the first time a doctor was present at the delivery, although his presence made little difference. The son Priscilla delivered was weak and sickly and died two days later. Once again C.T. and Priscilla mourned for a lost son. The older girls felt the loss of their baby brother as well.

Despite the loss of another son, C.T.'s faith was undeterred, and since he was home in England, he decided to make that his mission field. With rest, his asthma had settled down. He arranged a series of meetings around the British Isles, where he could tell stories of his work in China and challenge his audience with the need for more missionaries to go there and proclaim the gospel. Everywhere he went, people flocked to hear the great cricketer who had given away his fortune to follow Christ.

While he was holding meetings in Wales, C.T. stayed with his cousin, Dollie Thomas. He persuaded Dollie to go to one of the meetings with him, but she was not impressed with his message, and she told him so on the way home.

"Really, C.T.," she chided him, "what an awful thing you said this afternoon. 'True religion is like smallpox! If you get it, you give it to others and it spreads.' What were you thinking, comparing religion to a disease?"

"Well, that is the way I see it," C.T. replied. "I am trying to present my message in a way the common people will understand. And they would understand that, don't you think?"

His question was met by a stony silence that lasted all the way back to Dollie's house. When they arrived there, Dollie had the maid make cocoa for her and C.T. When the cocoa was ready, she held out a cup of it to C.T., but he went on talking to her, totally ignoring the fact that she was offering him the drink. It did not take Dollie long to get annoyed at his rudeness.

C.T. smiled. "Well," he said, finally looking at the cup of cocoa Dollie was offering him. "That is exactly how you are treating God. He is holding out the gift of eternal life to you, and you are ignoring the offer."

"I have never heard such a thing," Dollie said, putting the cup and saucer down on a nearby table before turning and storming out of the room.

The two of them did not have any more conversations about religion after that, but C.T. prayed that Dollie would respond to the gospel.

Two days later, when C.T. returned to London, a telegram was waiting for him. It read simply, "Got the smallpox badly—Dollie."

C.T. continued his speaking tour of the British Isles until 1896, when he was invited to cross the Atlantic Ocean and speak to students in the United States. He welcomed the opportunity, and in October that year he left Priscilla, who was still not well, and the girls in his mother's care and set off for what would become an eighteen-month tour.

During his time in the United States, C.T. often spoke in meetings five or six times a day. He also conducted thousands of private interviews with individual students. He wrote to Priscilla regularly, and often included newspaper clippings about his meetings, though he was not always pleased with the way the articles represented him.

One of the newspaper articles gushed about C.T.'s dedication to missions and the amazing sacrifices he had made. In the margin C.T. scribbled to Priscilla, "This is the kind of rot they write in the papers. One day a man got up and said something like this just before I spoke, so I got up and said, 'If I had known this was going to be said, I would have come a quarter hour later. Let's bow and wash it out in some prayer.'"

Over Christmas C.T. traveled through Nebraska and Kentucky on his speaking tour. In January he spoke at colleges in Pennsylvania and Ohio. He loved challenging the people who came to hear him to surrender everything to Christ. He wrote to Priscilla, "This life is just lovely. Everywhere souls are lighting up. God has prepared them."

When C.T. finally returned to England in April 1898, he found Priscilla ill and depressed. She had done her best to raise the children during the time he was away, but the nanny and C.T.'s mother made the job difficult for her. C.T. and Priscilla had very definite ideas about how they planned to live their lives and raise their children. It was a life in which the focus was not on material possessions or even on education but on obeying God's Word. But living in such a wealthy household, with rich cousins coming and going, pulled the girls toward the pleasures of a materialistic lifestyle.

This situation greatly disturbed C.T. and Priscilla, who both began to long for the missionary life, where their daughters would be far from such worldly influences. It was not surprising that when C.T. learned of an opportunity to go to India, he jumped at it. Mr. Vincent, C.T.'s father's old friend, offered to pay for C.T. to go to Tirhoot in North India, where C.T.'s father had made his fortune. Since C.T. had become a Christian, he had dreamed of going to India to preach the gospel to the natives who served on his father's indigo plantations, and now he had the opportunity to do so.

C.T. set out for India alone, with the understanding that when he found a place to settle, Priscilla and the girls would join him. As usual, C.T. made quite an impression when he arrived in British-run India. There were few English people, or expatriates, as they were called, who had not followed his cricketing career and had not wondered what had happened to him over the years.

They need wonder no more. C.T. enthusiastically spoke with everyone he met, Indians and English alike. He took an interpreter and went to the indigo plantations his father had owned to talk with the workers. He was delighted to find that many of the older workers remembered his father.

While he was in Tirhoot, C.T. heard of a group called the Anglo-Indian Evangelization Society, whose work he felt immediately drawn to. The society's function involved working among the expatriates who were often isolated from Christian fellowship or teaching. Through his contacts with the group, C.T. learned of an opening to pastor a Union Church in the hill country of southern India. The town where the church was located was called Ootacamund, or Ooty, as everyone called it. Ooty was a haven for expatriates: army personnel, government officials, and businessmen. These people all flocked to the cooler climate and mountain air as a refuge from the sweltering summer heat of the plains below. Ooty was 7,500 feet above sea level, and its climate resembled that of England in summer.

C.T. investigated the position further and found that a home and a salary came with the job. He also found that two-thirds of the pastor's time was to be spent in Ooty, while the other third was to be spent visiting English people in remote locations. This suited C.T. fine, and he applied for the job.

It was an exciting day in May when C.T. learned that he would be the next pastor of the Union Church in Ootacamund. He immediately wrote to Priscilla, telling her to pack up their belongings and bring the children to India.

Priscilla and the children arrived in Ooty in October 1900, along with a governess, who had been employed by C.T.'s mother. For the first time in five years, the Studd family were living together as a single unit. C.T. watched as the girls delighted in the new freedom away from their relatives' gaze. By now the oldest child, Grace, was nearly twelve years old, and the youngest, Pauline, was six.

As he watched his daughters, C.T. became painfully aware of how much of their childhood he had missed out on, and he tried to make it up to them. He and the girls took part in all of the events at Ooty, which included golf, horseback riding, polo, tennis, and of course, cricket. It was not long before C.T. had regained his old form and was batting double centuries, a feat that had been achieved only once before in India. When a cricket match was over, C.T. would invite the young Englishmen, many of them army officers, back to his house to talk about Christianity. Often they talked so late into the evening that the men had to spend the night at the Studd house.

So many conversions followed as a result of these conversations that visitors to Ooty were warned, "Don't go to the Union Church unless you want to get converted!" This was exactly the way C.T. liked things, and he was especially pleased when his own daughters came to him and asked to be baptized.

The problem C.T. had was where to baptize the girls, since none of the streams or rivers around Ooty were deep enough to use for a baptism. Finally C.T. came up with a solution. He ordered the gardener to dig up one of the flower beds to a depth of about four feet. Once the hole was dug, C.T. went to town and bought a huge, zinc-lined shipping crate, which he placed in the hole. On the morning of the baptism, the zinc-lined box was filled with water. It was a particularly cold day, and many kettles of boiling water were brought from the house to make the water in the makeshift baptistery tepid. However, the box leaked, and water had to be constantly added to it to maintain the water level.

A number of missionaries and Christian friends, among them Amy Carmichael, who ran a thriving mission in Dohnavur, at the southern tip of India, gathered to witness the baptism. Amy asked the girls many questions about the faith and their desire to be baptized and told C.T. how impressed she was with their answers. After the baptism everyone moved inside the Studd house, where they held a communion service.

Everything about living in Ootacamund was wonderful, except for one thing. The damp, cool climate that attracted so many people to the town was exactly the wrong climate for someone with asthma. At first C.T. was not greatly affected by it, but as the years went by, his asthma began to flare up once again. In fact, it got so bad that Priscilla wrote home describing C.T. as a "wreck." C.T. had to give up playing cricket, and he puffed and wheezed when walking even the short distance from his house to the church. Eventually, he had to face the fact that he was too ill to continue his duties as pastor. As well, by 1906 the girls had been through three governesses, each one sent out from England by C.T.'s mother, and a fourth could not be found. This combined with C.T.'s broken health made him start to think about going home. As he prayed about it, C.T. realized that his time in India was over.

As Priscilla helped him onto the steamer bound for England, C.T. had no idea what the future held. He asked himself if at forty-six this was the end of his missionary service. Would his health improve enough for him to continue with the work he loved?

Chapter 9

For Want of a Christian Missionary

Back in London the Studd family once again settled in with C.T.'s mother. She was an old woman by now and glad to have the company of her four lively granddaughters. However, they did not stay with her for long. C.T.'s sister, Dora, and her husband, Willie Bradshaw, offered to send the three oldest girls off to school in Switzerland, where it was hoped that they could make up for time lost in India. C.T. and Priscilla thought this was a good plan, and so they sent Grace, Edith, and Dorothy away to school.

The girls' departure meant that Priscilla was under less stress and C.T. could recuperate from his asthma. Sure enough, with rest, C.T.'s asthma began to settle down, and as soon as he was well enough,

C.T. began traveling and preaching again. Everyone, from police institutes to the YMCA and Wesleyan chapels, seemed to want him to speak. C.T. accepted every invitation he could possibly fit into his schedule, and over the course of the next two years, he challenged tens of thousands of English people to respond to the gospel and to take up the challenge of becoming missionaries.

Even the secular press lauded C.T.'s straightforward way of speaking. At the end of one of his meetings at Handsworth, C.T. challenged his audience by saying,

> We Christians today are indeed a tepid crew. Had we but half the fire and enthusiasm of the Suffragettes of the past, we would have the world evangelized.... Had we the pluck and heroism of the men who go on Polar expeditions or climb Everest, or for any ordinary daredevil enterprise, we could have every soul on earth knowing the name of Jesus Christ in less than ten years. To your knees, man! And to your Bible. Decide at once. Don't hedge. Time flies, cease your insults to God. Quit consulting flesh and blood. Stop your lame lying and cowardly excuses.

Reporting on this meeting, a Birmingham newspaper wrote,

> Mr. Studd is a missionary to emulate. And so all that band of college men from Handsworth thought as they cheered him to the echo, this man with the red tie and slim athletic body and young face. After more than twenty years in the harness he is bubbling over with life and humor; no pessimism about him, no lukewarmness; he loves and he follows, he teaches what he believes, he keeps a brave sunshiny face through it all. No subtleties appear to puzzle him; his faith is as brave as his speech is clear and straight.

Soon so many people were asking for copies of C.T.'s teachings that he compiled them into a booklet, which he entitled *The Chocolate Soldier.* The booklet encouraged Christian men and women not to melt like chocolate when times got hard but to press on with God. The book was an instant success.

The girls lasted eighteen months at school in Switzerland before they convinced their father that they would never master the French language. C.T. allowed them to come home and enroll in Sherborne School, one of the best girls' schools in England. Once again Dora and Willie generously paid for their nieces' tuition.

Whenever possible, Priscilla would accompany C.T. on his tours. But as they traveled, both of them longed to be back on the mission field, even though this seemed unlikely. Still, C.T. hoped and prayed that God would allow him and Priscilla to go back to China. Over the years he had followed the lives of the other members of the Cambridge Seven. In 1900 Cecil Polhill-Turner had returned to England because of ill health. Montagu Beauchamp had been evacuated during the Boxer Rebellion but was now back working in China. And Dixon Hoste was now director of the China Inland Mission. He had taken over the position when Hudson Taylor resigned as director.

By 1908 C.T. had toured England so many times that he was wondering what his future held. He seriously considered returning to India and living on the plains, where the climate would be better for his asthma. That is, he did until one particular day in Liverpool, where he was preaching. After lunch, as he strolled down the main street of the city, he noticed in the window of a building a large placard that read: "Cannibals want missionaries." *I am sure they do! Missionaries must be as tasty as anyone else,* C.T. laughed to himself. But his interest had been aroused, and he decided to go inside and see who had put up the placard.

Inside he was directed into a large meeting room, where a man with a thick German accent was speaking. C.T. recognized him immediately; it was Dr. Karl Kumm. Dr. Kumm was well known in England as the missionary who had walked across Africa. C.T. took off his hat and slipped into a seat at the back of the room.

"When I reached the middle of the continent," Dr. Kumm was saying, "I came across a number of tribes who had never heard the story of Jesus Christ. I asked one of the chiefs if he had ever seen a white person before, and he said that he had seen many of us. Some were big-game hunters, others were traders, officials, and scientists, but not one of them had ever been Christian enough to tell them the good news. My friends, we have to go soon. The Muslims are sweeping down from the north with their false religion, and no one is speaking up for Christ."

Karl Kumm's words sank deep into C.T.'s heart. C.T. prayed silently, *Lord, why have no Christians gone?*

He felt God reply to him, *Why don't you go?*

The doctor won't allow it, C.T. said, continuing the inner dialogue.

Am I not the Good Physician? Can I not see you through and keep you there? the voice came back.

There was nothing more to say; out of the blue, C.T. felt a clear challenge to go to Africa. It did not matter that he was forty-eight years old and in poor health and had no money. Somehow he knew he had to go to the continent known as the White Man's Grave.

When the meeting was over, C.T. spoke with Dr. Kumm, and the two men decided to travel together across northern Africa from east to west. They planned to preach and check out sites for mission stations along the way.

C.T. returned to London with a new purpose for his life—evangelizing Africa! But he met a wall of resistance when he mentioned his new goal to his wife and his mother. His mother could hardly believe her ears. As soon as she was convinced that her son was serious about this new venture, she burst into tears and pleaded with him to be more sensible.

Priscilla was just as horrified. "How could you?" she sobbed. "This will break up the family, and you will never survive out there."

But C.T. was unmoved. He had felt God's call to Africa, and that held all his thoughts captive. To his disappointment, his body did not cooperate, and he was too sick to leave England. He was in bed with a raging fever when Dr. Kumm set sail alone for Africa.

C.T. was devastated, but there was little he could do. He simply did not have the strength to climb out of bed and pack his clothes. His wife and mother hugged each other, assured that their prayers had been answered.

Life continued on in the Studd household. Dorothy was courted by and then married Gilbert Barclay, and the two of them moved to the north of England, where Gilbert became the pastor of a church. A year later Grace followed Dorothy's example. She married an elderly widower named Martin Sutton and moved to a luxurious home called Wargrave Manor.

After he recovered from his sickness, C.T. continued to travel around the British Isles, preaching two or three times a day. However, at the World Missionary Conference held in Edinburgh, Scotland, in 1910, his faith was stirred again. John R. Mott was one of the speakers at the conference. As a young man, he had been converted as a result of Kinny Studd's evangelistic tour of the United States, and he now led the Student Christian Movement. One of the messages John delivered at the conference was titled "Carrying the Gospel to All the Non-Christian World." John's words deeply impacted C.T., and they were only reinforced when Karl Kumm took the podium. Dr. Kumm had just returned from Africa, and once again he challenged his audience.

"There are twenty-six separate tribes who have not been evangelized yet," he said forcefully. "They range in size from five thousand members to two million. These tribes, which are along the borders of central Africa, stand in the way of the advance of Islam. It will be to our eternal shame if, for want of a Christian missionary, these people are converted to Islam."

Once again C.T. felt the call to Africa.

The conference speakers inspired many others besides C.T., and by the end of the gathering, a group of businessmen had formed themselves into a committee to financially back missionaries who wanted to go to the tribes in Africa that were unreached with the gospel. The committee agreed to pay C.T.'s expenses so that he could go to Africa with Dr. Kumm. However, they put one condition on their support: C.T. must pass a medical examination.

Plans for the trip were quickly made, and a sailing date set. But as the departure date got nearer,

C.T. dragged his feet on getting a medical exam. Finally the committee told him he had to go to a doctor, and so he did. The results, though, were not what he wanted to hear. The doctor agreed that it might be all right for C.T. to visit the north of the African continent. But under no circumstances, he warned, should C.T. travel south of Khartoum, Sudan, as that area was renowned for severe cases of malaria and sleeping sickness. C.T., however, could not make such a promise, and so the committee withdrew its support of him.

C.T. was resolute. If need be, he would go to Africa alone and make a survey of the areas that still needed missionaries. At the next meeting of the committee, C.T. told them, "Gentlemen, God has called me to go, and I will go. I will blaze the trail, though my grave may only be a stepping-stone that younger men may follow. Jesus tells us that 'he that shall lose his life for My sake and the gospel's shall find it,' and I, if I lose my life following Jesus, so be it."

The ship on which C.T. was due to sail to Africa departed in just three weeks, but C.T. had no money to pay for the ticket. He told no one that the committee had withdrawn its support of him, and he chose instead to continue his farewell tour, trusting that God would supply the money some other way. With two weeks to go, C.T. preached at the Linnacre Mission in Liverpool. As always, he never took an offering or asked for money when he spoke, but after the service a stranger pressed a ten-pound note into his hand. It was not enough to pay his way to

Africa, but it was a start. Over the next two weeks, more money flowed in from the most unexpected sources, and soon C.T. had the money to pay for his ticket to Africa.

Priscilla and C.T.'s mother were still upset about C.T.'s leaving, but they had grown used to the idea in the two years that had passed since he first suggested it. C.T. reminded his wife of the pledge they had made to each other on their wedding day twenty-two years before: "We will never hinder one another from serving Thee." He explained to Priscilla as gently as he could that God had called him to Africa, and he could not turn aside from that call. He also told her that he did not want her to come along, because he feared the many dangerous situations that most certainly lay ahead. The journey would be difficult for one person in weak health, he reasoned, but for two people in weak health, it would be impossible to accomplish the goals of the trip. C.T. felt he would need to be free to move as he felt directed by God.

On December 15, 1910, C.T. set sail aboard the SS *Warwickshire,* bound for Africa. It was a cold, gloomy day, and it matched his mood. It had been excruciatingly difficult to leave his family with no idea whether or when he would see them again.

Aboard ship C.T. sat at a table in the salon and prayed that God would comfort him in the turmoil he felt about leaving his family. As he prayed, the most astonishing thought ran through his mind. "This trip is not merely for the Sudan," a voice seemed to be saying to him. "It is for the whole unevangelized world."

C.T. shook his head. It seemed ridiculous that one fifty-year-old man, heading to the Sudan with little backing and no fellow missionaries, could alter the course of mission history! Yet as the voyage continued, C.T. could not forget the words. It was as if they were etched into his mind.

On the trip C.T. sent letters home to Priscilla from every port the ship stopped at. Knowing that this trip represented a huge sacrifice on her part, he hoped she would find comfort in the excitement of what he was certain lay ahead. On December 20 he brought his writing materials up to the salon and sat down at a desk to write to Priscilla.

> Somehow God tells me all my life has been a preparation for this coming ten years or more. It has been a rough discipline. Oh, the agony of it! The asthma, what has not that meant, a daily and nightly dying! The bodily weakness! The being looked down upon by the world folk! The poverty! And have I not been tempted? Tempted to stop working for Christ! Doctors! Relatives! Family! Christians!

He looked out at the steel gray horizon for a few minutes before continuing.

> Things simply surge through my mind and head, and God speaks to me every time I lie

> down, and assures me that He is going to do a wonderful work. Darling Priscilla, you remember Shanghai? Well, those days are going to occur again, only on a magnificent scale. Oh, this New Crusade, it burns in my brain and heart. It must be.

Then in January, as the SS *Warwickshire* approached the coast of Africa, C.T. wrote another heart-to-heart letter to his wife.

> Let us in our old age reconsecrate ourselves to Jesus. He has done so much for us.... He has kept us going, and kept our girls and saved them. God grant that as a silver wedding present He may give us this noble work to do for Him in Africa.... Seldom in a life do two people have the opportunity to forsake all twice, but we are being offered this privilege. Let us grasp it with both hands.

Chapter 10

Africa at Last

Ready and eager to scout for mission stations across the African continent, C.T. Studd stepped off the SS *Warwickshire* in Mombasa, Kenya. From Mombasa he made his way to Nairobi, where he stayed with a Christian family to whom Karl Kumm had provided a letter of introduction. In Nairobi he began gathering maps and information about the Sudan, the great swath of land that stretched some twenty-five hundred miles across Africa south of the Sahara Desert, between the Niger River in the west and the Nile in the east. C.T. spent his days poring over the maps, many of them vague about the exact geography of the region, and visiting church leaders in Nairobi to find out just how many mission stations and churches they knew of in the Sudan.

Finally, six weeks after arriving in Kenya, C.T. was ready to set out. He had convinced Bishop Gwynne and Archdeacon Shaw, both of the Church Mission Society (CMS), to be his traveling companions. Their plan was to travel north to Khartoum and from there undertake a nine-hundred-mile trek to the southwest through a region called Bahr al Ghazal. Accompanying C.T. and his two traveling companions were ten porters and twenty-nine donkeys laden with provisions for the trip.

It was the rainy season when they set out, and progress was slow. Still, C.T., Bishop Gwynne, and Archdeacon Shaw made the most of every opportunity. They preached whenever they found a tribe willing to listen and made copious notes about what they found in the region. However, as the trek proceeded, C.T. got the distinct feeling he was headed in the wrong direction. The area they were traveling through was sparsely populated, and it seemed to him that with some organization, the CMS could easily evangelize the whole Bahr al Ghazal area themselves.

C.T. wondered where the great masses of unsaved Africans he had heard so much about were located. As he talked to people along the route of their journey, he learned that the masses he sought were beyond the southern frontier of the Sudan in the Belgian Congo, where, he was told, lived millions of destitute people who had never heard the gospel. Before the journey through Bahr al Ghazal was over, C.T. knew he was destined to work in the Congo.

After ten weeks of traveling, the group straggled back into Khartoum. Only five donkeys had survived the trek, and several of the porters had defected along the way. But C.T. was happy. He had enjoyed wonderful health the entire time, a sign, he was sure, that God wanted him to start a mission in the Belgian Congo. His plan was to return to England and gather a small group of dedicated daredevils to come back to Africa with him. But those plans had to wait. Within days of returning to Khartoum, C.T. came down with a severe attack of malaria. He lay on his bed for eight weeks before he felt well enough to travel back to England.

C.T. was still weak when he arrived in England, and almost everyone he met criticized him for going to Africa in the first place. He spent most of the summer of 1911 recuperating, but even as his body rested, his mind was alive with ideas.

C.T. kept a notebook and pencil beside him at all times. As the days went by, the outline of a very different mission society began to take shape in his notebook. C.T. decided that there were enough mission organizations to support "regular" missionaries. What he wanted to do was attract and train a group of young men who would go into the most dangerous places on earth with no thought to their personal safety. They would be a union mission made up of many denominations, blazing a trail that other mission societies could follow. C.T. scribbled down a mission statement for the new mission:

> For this purpose we have banded ourselves together under the name of "Christ's Etceteras," and invite others of God's people to join us in this glorious enterprise.... We rejoice in and thank God for the good work being carried on in the already occupied lands by God's Regular Forces. We seek to attack and win to Christ only those parts of the devil's empire which are beyond the extremest outposts of the regular army of God. Christ's Etceteras are a union mission; a Christian, and, therefore, an international brotherhood; a supplementary Worldwide Evangelization Crusade.

As soon as he was well enough, C.T. took to the road with his new ideas. He had decided to call the new mission the Heart of Africa Mission, or H.A.M. for short. He was gratified to learn that the English public had not forgotten their old sports hero, and as before, huge crowds came out to hear him speak.

At the meetings C.T. had only one message for his audience. "Five hundred millions of heathen have not yet been evangelized, so it is computed," he would tell the crowd. "The heart of Asia, the heart of Africa, and well nigh the entire continent of South America, are untouched with the gospel of Christ. Yes, we shout, 'Onward Christian soldiers, marching as to war,' and then?...then?...we whisper, 'I pray Thee have me excused.' What glorious humbugs we are! We have been waiting far too long for someone else to get the job. The time for waiting is past. The hour of God has struck. War is declared! Didn't Christ Himself tell us that the gates of hell should not prevail against us? What have men like us got to fear? Before the whole world, yes, before the sleepy, lukewarm, faithless, namby-pamby Christian world, we must dare to trust our God, to venture our all for Him."

As a result of C.T.'s numerous speaking engagements, twenty-four young men volunteered to return to the Belgian Congo with C.T. The desire of one of these young men to go to the Congo strained the relationship between C.T. and one of his oldest friends. C.T. and Barclay Buxton had first met while they were students at Cambridge. Barclay came from a wealthy family, and he shocked everyone when he and his wife, their estate carpenter, and two housemaids set out for Japan to start a mission. The mission became known as the "Japan Band," and now, even though Barclay and his family were back in England, Barclay still supported other Japan Band workers.

Barclay's second son, Alfred, was a tall, thin twenty-year-old studying at Cambridge University to become a doctor. He was also courting Edith Studd, C.T.'s daughter. When Alfred heard C.T. speak, he was immediately captivated with the idea of going to Africa as a missionary. He wanted to leave right away with C.T. for Africa, but his parents called it a harebrained scheme. His father refused to allow him to go, frustrating Alfred and straining the relationship between Barclay and C.T. But Alfred's conviction that he should go to Africa with C.T. would not leave him. Eventually Barclay relented, although he was less than enthusiastic about Alfred's dropping out of medical school to venture into such a dangerous place.

Alfred's father was not the only person who thought C.T.'s plan was crazy. Priscilla and the girls also hated to see him return to Africa. Priscilla was particularly upset because it would mean staying with her mother-in-law indefinitely. As C.T. prayed about Priscilla's situation, he became convinced that they should buy their own home in London for her to live in while he was away in Africa. Soon C.T. heard about a house at 17 Highland Road, Norwood, London. He went to see the place and liked what he saw. The house was modest but adequate, and best of all, it was a great bargain. C.T. borrowed some money and bought the place. Priscilla was overjoyed to be moving into her own house and soon had it furnished.

Once Priscilla had settled in, C.T. felt free to return to Africa and blaze a trail for the young men who had committed themselves to join him there. Three of the young men from Cambridge were already in Mombasa, awaiting C.T.'s arrival. Alfred Buxton would accompany C.T. on the voyage to Kenya.

On January 31, 1913, C.T. spent his last night at home. He and Alfred were due to set sail the following morning. After dinner that night, a young man came by to say farewell to C.T., but as they spoke, the young man became agitated about the situation.

"You are fifty-two years old," he said. "How could you leave your country, your home, your wife, and your daughters?"

C.T. thought for a moment and then said, "If Jesus Christ be God and died for me, then no sacrifice can be too great for me to make for Him!"

Something about that phrase struck C.T., and before he went to bed that night, he wrote it down in his journal. He reminded himself that sacrificing everything was reasonable when he looked at things from heaven's perspective.

The following morning C.T. and Alfred boarded the ship. They were an unlikely pair. One was considered by most people to be too old to embark on such a missionary endeavor, and the other was considered too young for it.

It was a difficult farewell, especially for Edith Studd, who had become engaged to Alfred the week before.

As dusk fell on the first day at sea, C.T. wrote a letter to Priscilla.

> I longed, but dared not, say good-bye or kiss again. I dared not. The tears came as I thought of your tears, and tears again of joy at the way He comforted you. Now let

> us thank Him in anticipation not only with our lips but by our lives. You little dream of how I know that you pay the greatest price, only I did not dare say so to you, but I do admire you, darling, and shall ever do so.... I have never felt the power of God more since those Shanghai days. Truly this has been like the Seven going out. Good-bye, my darling Priscilla. We began risking all for God and we will end as we began, loving each other utterly and only less than we love Jesus.

The voyage to Kenya was uneventful, and the two men arrived in Africa in good spirits. But no sooner had they disembarked than the problems began.The three young men who had gone on ahead met them in Mombasa, and they confessed that they were having serious doubts about going on to the Congo with C.T. Many Christians in Mombasa and Nairobi had told them that they thought C.T.'s ideas were unrealistic and that his health was not up to living in Africa.

This was a great blow to C.T., who had been looking forward to the five of them joining forces and traveling on to the Congo. Now he wondered whether he should go on with Alfred as his sole companion. He even feared that if Alfred talked to the other three, he, too, would have reservations about going on.

During the voyage to Africa, C.T. and Alfred had become good friends, and after listening to what the other three had to say, Alfred decided to journey on with C.T. Fearing that Alfred's resolve might falter if they waited in Mombasa too long, C.T. was anxious to get moving. He hastily bought all the supplies he thought they would need, including two bicycles. Then he and Alfred said good-bye to the three young men and traveled to Nairobi. From Nairobi they caught a train and headed westward to Lake Victoria. There they transferred to a steamer and crossed the lake before boarding another train. After another steamer ride across another lake and then a car ride over deeply rutted roads, they finally reached Masindi, a small CMS mission station in Uganda.

C.T. and Alfred arrived in Masindi exhausted. Since there was no room for them in the mission house, they pitched their tent in the yard, facing the door toward the west. Beyond the mission station to the west lay a large, unmapped area populated with lions, snakes, and cannibals! C.T. was on the verge of fulfilling the dream he had nurtured since reading the placard "Cannibals want missionaries" in Liverpool five years before.

The following morning C.T. awoke feeling refreshed and ready to keep moving. He soon became concerned for Alfred, however, who had developed a high fever in the night and was too weak to get out of bed. C.T. nursed and spoon-fed his friend. Since arriving in Africa, Alfred had lost a lot of weight, and C.T. began to worry about his condition. A nagging voice in his head said, *We are still in British East Africa. How will he cope when we reach the real fever zone?* It was a question C.T. could not answer.

C.T. and Alfred had been camped at Masindi for three days when a telegram arrived from London for Alfred. It had been sent on from Mombasa, and C.T. hoped it would cheer him up. Most likely it was a note of encouragement from his father. But Alfred's mouth dropped open as he read the telegram. It was not what he or C.T. had been expecting. The telegram read, "Cannot consent you two going interior alone."

C.T. could scarcely believe it. Was this the end of the trip into the Belgian Congo?

Chapter 11

Lunch with Cannibals

Before he could open his mouth and say the wrong thing, C.T. groaned and quickly left the tent. He dare not try to persuade Alfred to carry on. While C.T. was ready to face disease, wild animals, and hostile natives himself, he would not force another man to do the same. If, after receiving the telegram from his father, Alfred wanted to return to Nairobi, so be it. The situation was made all the more difficult because Alfred was no ordinary traveling companion; he was the son of C.T.'s good friend and his daughter's fiancé.

I will have to wait and pray that God will make Alfred's path clear to him, C.T. told himself as he left the tent.

The following morning Alfred's temperature was back to normal, and his eyes were shining with anticipation. "I have made up my mind," he told C.T. "We will face the future together, whatever it may hold."

"Are you quite sure you have heard from God on this?" C.T. asked.

"Yes," Alfred replied. "In fact, I spent much of the night meditating on Psalm 105. Here, listen to this. 'When they were but a few men in number; yea, very few, and strangers in it. When they went from one nation to another, from one kingdom to another people; he suffered no man to do them wrong: yea, he reproved kings for their sakes; saying, Touch not mine anointed, and do my prophets no harm.' C.T., I believe we are to go forward together and that God will take care of us. It is past time for the gospel to advance into the heart of Africa. I for one want to be a part of that."

C.T. brushed a tear from his eye. "Bless you for your loyalty, my boy," he said. "It is settled then. As soon as you are well enough, we will begin the three-day trek to Lake Albert.

That night, though, they suffered another setback. One of the porters was lighting a candle when a gust of wind blew the flame toward the canvas tent, which immediately caught fire. C.T. heard a loud whoosh and turned to see the roaring flames. He sprang to his feet and yelled for everyone to stand clear. Then he watched helplessly as the tent and everything in it was engulfed by the fire and destroyed.

The following morning, as C.T. stood looking at the pile of embers that was once their tent and belongings, the thought that they could go back for more supplies crossed his mind. But C.T. refused to entertain it—retreat was not in his vocabulary. Instead he decided that they would press on with the smaller tents and the supplies they still had. God would make up the shortfall, he was sure of that.

The porters had lighter burdens to bear as the group set out the following morning. The group headed west and, after three days of trekking, arrived at the eastern shore of Lake Albert. C.T. stopped and took off his cap. In the hazy distance, across the lake, he could see land—the Belgian Congo. He felt like Joshua preparing to enter the Promised Land. An overwhelming feeling of gratitude overcame him—gratitude to God for his health and strength, gratitude to Alfred for his loyalty and faith, and gratitude to all those in England who had made this moment possible through their prayer and financial support.

Alfred walked up behind C.T. and took in the view himself. The two of them then sank to their knees. "Father, we are Yours," C.T. prayed. "Give us favor with the government officials. Help us to get entry into the land. Show us where to go; direct our paths."

When they finished praying, they stood up, and C.T. asked Alfred if he spoke any French.

"Just the bit I learned at school," Alfred replied.

"We ought to be able to manage with that," C.T. laughed. "So many people have said that the Belgians won't let British people through their territory, but when they hear your French, they'll probably welcome us and let us do anything we want."

That night the men camped on the lakeshore. Since food supplies were running low, they ate porridge for dinner. They were just finishing it when a white man, obviously a trader, paddled up in a canoe.

"Hall's the name," the man yelled. "Are you British?"

"We certainly are," C.T. replied. "Come and sit with us."

The trader pulled his canoe up onto the sandy shore and strolled over to C.T. and Alfred. He was carrying a welcome string of fish. Soon the fish were frying over the open fire while Hall busily talked away.

"I only stay on the British side of the lake," he said. "And the likes of you would too if you have any sense."

"What makes you say that?" Alfred asked.

Hall laughed. "I've seen too much to ever want to get tangled up in the Belgian Congo. Last month an English adventurer was stripped and beaten and sent back across the lake more dead than alive. But he recovered, not like the elephant hunter who was shot in the shoulder with a poisoned arrow. He's buried over there in the jungle. No. If you enter the Congo, you'll never come out alive."

"Oh, they'll be too interested in our bicycles to do anything to us," C.T. said, pointing to the two bicycles that lay beside the tent.

"Bicycles!" the trader exclaimed. "You can't be serious. You don't mean to bicycle through the jungle, do you?"

"That's precisely what we intend to do. And when they can't carry us, we'll carry them," C.T. replied.

"Now I've heard everything!" Hall said, shaking his head. "I hope you two both have wills written, because you are going to need them."

"We will trust ourselves into God's hands," C.T. said. "We're on His mission, and He will see us through."

The trader shrugged. "So you are taking the steamer to Mahagi tomorrow then, I expect."

"We hope so," Alfred said. "We hear that some missionaries from another agency have set up a camp there, and we hope to get some information from them, but ultimately we are headed for Dungu."

Hall whistled. "Rather you than me!"

That night C.T. did not sleep well. Rain and wind battered the tent, and he found himself replaying the trader's words. Of course, to the natural eyes, it was suicide to go into the Congo, but C.T. refused to be a "chocolate soldier"—if it cost him his life to follow orders, so be it.

The next day the men broke camp and took the steamer across Lake Albert to Mahagi. Much of the way across, C.T. prayed for favor with the Belgian immigration officials they would meet on the other side. His prayers were answered. Even though they were a two-man mission with no one else to back them, the officials welcomed C.T. and Alfred and wished them luck in their travels.

"You are going to need it!" one of the officials said. "Pray you don't meet the Balenda tribe. They are in an uproar right now and likely to dismember a strange white man on the spot."

"Thank you," C.T. said, quickly gathering up his papers. He did not want to stay and hear more discouraging information.

The trip westward started out smoothly enough. Their first stop along the route was to be Kilo, some eighty miles away. The bicycles proved to be a useful way to get around. They were faster than walking and easier on the feet. However, C.T. and Alfred were only two days into the trek when they found themselves far ahead of their porters.

When they came to a fork in the trail they were following, C.T. and Alfred decided to take the fork that continued west. Kilo lay to the west, and since the other fork headed in a more northerly direction, they reasoned the westerly fork was the right one to take. Regrettably, they were wrong. Soon the track they had chosen to follow petered out, and the two missionaries found themselves lost in the dense African jungle.

C.T. and Alfred tried to find the way back to the trail. They stumbled over large tree roots in the steamy, dense jungle while monkeys scurried around in the branches above their heads. But their attempt to find their way back only led them deeper into the jungle. Disoriented and by now very hungry, they came to a small clearing. They emerged from the sunless gloom of the jungle into bright sunlight. C.T. studied the sky above, searching for a cloud, a migrating bird, anything that might help him get his bearing. But still he had no idea how to rejoin the trail.

All the warnings other Europeans had given C.T. and Alfred about the dangers of the area rushed into their minds. Both had the uneasy sensation of being watched. C.T. shivered as he stared into the dense foliage surrounding them. He and Alfred were exposed on all sides, clearly visible to anything or anyone concealed in the jungle.

At the sound of a rustle in the foliage behind them, both men spun around in time to see an African man emerge into the sunlight. C.T.'s and Alfred's eyes were drawn to the bow and arrows the man held in his left hand. The man smiled, but the smile did not put the missionaries at ease. Instead it revealed teeth that had been filed to sharp points—a sure sign of cannibalism.

"I hope he is not one of the Balenda people they told us about at the border," Alfred remarked.

"Yes," C.T. agreed.

Only then did C.T. see the basket of sweet potatoes and maize the man was carrying in his right hand. The man, wearing only a tattered shirt, was still smiling. Deciding that he meant them no harm,

C.T. used gestures to indicate that he and Alfred were hungry. The African readily came closer and gave C.T. some of the vegetables in his basket. When C.T. offered him some buttons in return, a broad smile spread across the man's face, his sharpened teeth glistening in the sunlight. Then, suddenly, he beckoned for the two missionaries to follow him as he set off into the jungle. C.T. and Alfred looked at each other, then picked up their bicycles and followed.

C.T. and Alfred followed the man for an hour until they came to another clearing. In this clearing sat a cluster of grass huts. Smoke rose from a fire, and children ran around chasing one another. But as soon as they saw two white men in their village, they stopped playing and gathered round C.T. and Alfred, smiling at them and revealing their sharpened cannibal teeth.

"Do you think this might be a trap and they're going to kill us and eat us?" Alfred asked, the fear obvious in his voice.

"No, I don't think so," came back C.T.'s calm voice. "There are more tender and appetizing animals to eat in the jungle."

The man led the missionaries to a fire near one of the grass huts. Once he was sure they were seated comfortably, he placed the sweet potatoes and ears of maize into the embers of the fire. Half an hour later, he pulled the vegetables from the embers and served them to C.T. and Alfred. He brought some cooked meat from inside the hut and served it to them as well. The two missionaries, famished after a day lost in the jungle, gobbled down the meat and vegetables. The sweet potatoes and maize were perfectly cooked, and the meat was tender and tasty. C.T. and Alfred weren't sure what animal the meat came from, and C.T. thought it better not to inquire.

When they had finished eating, C.T. tore some more buttons from his pants to pay for the food.

As C.T. and Alfred stood to leave, the African man seemed to sense that they were lost and turned and pointed into the jungle.

"I think he's telling us to go that way," C.T. told Alfred.

Both men shook the man's hand, picked up their bicycles, and headed in the direction the man had pointed. As they left, the people of the village gathered around and applauded the two missionaries. C.T. waved to them, and then he and Alfred disappeared into the dense jungle.

As they made their way along, C.T. prayed silently, thanking God for keeping them safe. They had survived their first encounter with cannibals. In fact, not only had they survived it, but also they had departed friends. Hall's dire warning on the eastern shore of Lake Albert two nights before and the words of the Belgian immigration officials at the border had proved unfounded, and C.T., for one, was happy about that.

On realizing that the missionaries might be lost, several of the porters had come into the jungle to look for them. As C.T. and Alfred made their way in the direction the man had pointed, they soon came upon the porters looking for them. By nightfall they were back on the right trail and pitching their tents in a clearing.

The next day the two men bicycled on toward Kilo, though C.T. kept a constant ear out for the sounds of the porters behind them.

Four days later, on June 5, C.T. and Alfred peddled into Kilo. They were no doubt the first people ever to do so, judging by the commotion their bicycles created among the inhabitants of the mining town. People lined up along the main street of the town and yelled and whistled as they watched the two missionaries balance on their strange machines with two wheels.

Soon a Greek trader stepped forward and introduced himself. He spoke in broken English, but his intentions were clear. He invited C.T. and Alfred and their porters to make camp in his compound, where they could stay until they were rested and ready to go on.

C.T. gratefully accepted the offer, assuming that they would be there for a night or two. He had no inkling that it would be three long, uncomfortable months before they would be on their way again.

Chapter 12

In the Heart of Africa

Mail was waiting for C.T. and Alfred at Kilo. The letters, delivered by a runner traveling faster than the missionary party could, contained good news. C.T. was now a grandfather. His daughter Dorothy had given birth to a girl, who had been named Ann. And Alfred's father wrote not only to apologize for the negative telegram he had sent his son but also to announce that Alfred's older brother George was preparing to join them in the Congo. C.T. was very relieved to hear the news. It meant not only that his friendship with Barclay Buxton was still intact but also that Alfred now had the full blessing of his father in his missionary endeavor.

The letters also contained some bad news. Priscilla wrote that her heart was failing. She had collapsed while out shopping, and the doctor had confined her to bed for most of the day. However, she was still doing what she could to help the mission. She had written a newsletter for the Heart of Africa Mission and had it printed on heart-shaped pages. About two thousand copies of the newsletter had been mailed out to interested people. Priscilla also informed C.T. that his new mission was being constantly criticized by Christians who thought he should work alongside an existing mission like the Africa Inland Mission, or AIM for short. To make matters worse, some of those criticizing C.T. were members of the Heart of Africa Mission board, which C.T. had set up before he left. Still, C.T. was grateful that two members of the board, his son-in-law Martin Sutton and his old friend Lord Radstock, stood staunchly behind his work and supported Priscilla any way they could.

C.T. wrote back immediately to Priscilla, encouraging her to look to "Dr. Jesus" to heal her. He added,

> We can trust Him too little, but we can never trust Him too much.... It is well to look things right in the eye and for God to try us like Gideon. When he has tried us to the utmost we shall come forth like gold. I really believe God has got us in tow and that He intends to execute His work of evangelizing the world. By God's grace I intend to be in the job for all I'm worth come life or come death, committee or no committee, helper or no helper.

Over the next three months, this statement was to be tested in C.T.'s life. The group of porters who had traveled with C.T. and Alfred to Kilo disbanded, and for the first time since C.T. and Alfred had been in Africa, they had difficulty forming a new team of porters and so couldn't continue their journey. In addition, little information had been available to C.T. and Alfred about the climate in the Belgian Congo, and what little they had read proved to be very misleading. The men had expected sunny, blue skies and sprinklings of rain. What they got in Kilo was deluges of rain and gusts of wind that lifted their tents off the ground and dashed them against the trees. Sometimes C.T. and Alfred sat in wet clothes for a week at a time, and when a storm hit, they had no shelter from its intense fury.

Despite the miserable conditions and the uncertainty of when they would be able to get enough porters to move on, the two men kept themselves busy. They rose around five o'clock in the morning and had a cup of tea. Then they read their Bibles separately until breakfast at eight. From nine until one in the afternoon, each man worked on his own projects. Alfred set about trying to learn the basics of Bangala, the local trade language, while C.T. wrote tracts and booklets that he sent home to Priscilla to be published. At one, C.T. and Alfred ate lunch and then prayed together. Much to his disgust, C.T. often had to take an afternoon nap, as he tired easily, a lingering effect of his bouts with malaria. After a nap he would work until five, when Alfred would join him for dinner. After dinner C.T. would stroll around town and return to camp in time to go to bed at nine.

The weeks turned into months, and finally, in late August, enough porters had been assembled for the missionaries to proceed with the final stage of their journey to Dungu. On August 28, 1913, C.T. was very glad to peddle out of Kilo and northwest into the Ituri forest.

The Ituri forest stretched on for miles over jagged mountains. The trees were so dense that they let little sunlight reach the forest floor. C.T., Alfred, and the porters made their way along in what seemed to them perpetual twilight. The trail they followed was narrow and treacherous, with large boulders and tree roots blocking their path. C.T. and Alfred soon found themselves carrying their bicycles more than they were riding. To make matters worse, the forest was continually damp. Water dripped from the branches above, causing slippery moss and lichen to grow over everything on the forest floor. At times it seemed to C.T. more like they were walking on ice than through an African jungle. C.T. and Alfred and the porters were constantly slipping and falling. C.T. wrote in his diary that the trail seemed like it was "soaped by the devil night and morning to ensure [its] being slippery."

After four days the porters had had enough. They laid down their burdens—camping equipment and boxes of food—and disappeared into the forest. C.T. could hardly believe it. He could do nothing else but send Alfred on down the track to the next Belgian government station, or poste, as the stations were called, to try to find some more porters. Alfred's ability to speak a little of the local language helped him hire some new porters, along with a few of the original ones who wanted to be paid more money before going back into the forest.

Finally, after eleven days of slipping and sliding, the men emerged into the sunlight once again. The grassland of Welle province now surrounded them, and the going was much easier. Soon they arrived at their next stopping place, the poste at Arebi. From there the path to Dungu was much easier for bicycling, and they made good progress. They passed many gardens along the way and were able to buy or trade for rice, millet, monkey nuts, bananas, sweet potatoes, and pineapples. It was a tropical feast to C.T., who could not think of when he had eaten so well.

Six weeks after leaving Kilo, the missionary party arrived at their destination, the unevangelized town of Dungu, or at least that is what C.T. thought when he entered the town. C.T. headed straight for the post office, where he received some disturbing news, not from the mail but from the postmaster.

As he handed C.T. several letters, the postmaster said, "So you are joining the other missionaries, are you?"

"What other missionaries? Surely we are the only missionaries here," C.T. replied.

The postmaster shook his head and looked down at a list. "No," he said, "there are four others. They arrived ten days ago and have already been granted land rights to start a mission. Let me see. Their names are Morris, Batstone, Miller, and Clarke."

C.T. was dumbfounded. He recognized the names of Morris and Batstone—two of the young men who had been waiting for him in Mombasa and then decided not to go with him. "What mission are they with, do you know?" he asked.

"I believe it is called AIM," the postmaster replied.

C.T. opened his mouth to say something and then closed it again. Instead he took the letters and walked out into the bright sunlight.

That night, as they made camp, C.T. wondered what to do. He had come to the heart of Africa to pioneer a mission to people who had no other chance of hearing the gospel, not to follow in the footsteps of other missionaries. In choosing Dungu, he was sure he had found a spot that would take other mission organizations years to reach, but apparently he had been wrong. He now wondered what he and Alfred should do next.

When C.T. went to speak to the four men, Morris and Batstone explained that after they had left C.T. in Mombasa, they had decided to join up with the Africa Inland Mission. The mission had two missionaries about to head into the Congo, and so the four men had joined together. They had taken a slightly different route from the one C.T. and Alfred had taken, and had not experienced the same delays. Thus they had started later and arrived earlier in Dungu.

After talking with the four young men, C.T. could see only one course of action. He and Alfred would proceed farther west to the town of Niangara, a place that everyone assured him had never hosted a missionary before.

Since their porters had already been paid and had left, C.T. and Alfred began the exhausting job of rounding up a new group. During this time they were invited to stay in the guest house of a Belgian merchant, and they gratefully accepted the offer. After spotting several black mambas, one of the most deadly snakes in Africa, they were glad for the protection of a house.

On their first night in the guest house, a terrible thunderstorm broke over Dungu. Thunder cracked and lightning illuminated the room where C.T. and Alfred knelt in prayer. Suddenly there was an enormous crash, and a chunk of plaster fell from the ceiling, landing beside C.T.'s leg. C.T. jumped up and rushed outside to see what was happening, Alfred close at his heels.

Sheets of rain drenched them both in seconds. C.T. looked up at the roof to see a thin plume of smoke coming from the thatch. Lightning had struck the house and set the roof alight. C.T. studied the roof for a moment, and then the two men raced back inside out of the rain. As he shut the door behind them, C.T. was convinced that the torrential rain would soon put the fire out. Meanwhile, a group of local people had gathered outside, and C.T. could hear them shouting above the din of the storm.

"What are they saying?" he asked Alfred.

Alfred gulped. "They're telling us to get our things and run."

The two men looked at each other for a second, and then some flaming thatch fell through the ceiling and landed next to a table. C.T. rushed over and stomped the fire out, but the crackling above his head told him there would be more fire raining down on them at any moment.

"Quick. Let's grab our belongings and get out of here," C.T. yelled to Alfred.

A minute later C.T. and Alfred were standing in the midst of the group of local people, watching as the guest house was engulfed in flames. For the second time, fire had stalked their journey.

As he stood watching, C.T. noticed a white man standing beside him. The man was wearing nothing but a towel around his waist. He introduced himself. "I am Count de Grunne, the Belgian district commissioner. Were you staying here?"

"Yes," C.T. replied.

"I came as soon as I heard about the fire," the commissioner said, "though I suppose you can see that!"

C.T. looked into the man's direct, gray eyes and liked him immediately.

"I suppose you will need another house for the night. I will have one of my servants prepare one for you right away," the commissioner offered.

"Thank you," C.T. replied. "That is very kind of you."

Over the next few days, Count de Grunne showed his kindness in many other ways. He helped C.T. and Alfred find more porters and granted them land at Niangara to build their mission station. He also gave them maps and advice on how to get to Niangara. He suggested that the easiest way to get there was to take canoes down the Welle River. In three days they would reach their destination. C.T. readily accepted the count's suggestion.

On October 16, 1913, C.T. and Alfred stepped out of their canoes and onto the riverbank at Niangara. After nine months of living mostly in tents, they were "home" at last. In no time at all, the two missionaries had built themselves a large house from mud and wattle and christened it "Buckingham Palace." Indeed, after the trials they had been through, they could not imagine anything more luxurious than solid walls around them and a waterproof roof over their heads.

On the first night in their new home, C.T. wrote in his journal, "We are the farthest outpost of God's work; there is nothing west, north or south of us, till you strike the Congo River."

That was just the way C.T. had always wanted things to be—he and Alfred deep in the heart of Africa.

As the next days unfolded, they found that Niangara was like the hub of a wheel. Around them lived many tribes, including the Bazande, Mangbetu, Medje, Nepoko, and Pygmies. C.T. was delighted; the possibilities for evangelization were even vaster than he had first thought.

Within days of arriving in Niangara, C.T. and Alfred set out to explore the area around them, looking for sites for potential mission stations. They decided to head south, despite the fact that only ten years before a band of thirty-five Belgian soldiers walking in that direction had all been killed, cooked, and eaten by cannibals.

No cannibals crossed their path on the journey, and after walking five days, they found a perfect spot for a mission station. Nala was an abandoned government poste that had a bountiful supply of food and water and several brick buildings that the local people did not use. More important, C.T. and Alfred were impressed by the friendliness of the people they met. Having been exposed to white people before, the residents of Nala were eager for someone to teach them to read and write and explain the outside world to them.

When they got back to Niangara, C.T. wasted no time in writing to the board of the Heart of Africa Mission. He explained the openness of the people at Nala and concluded, "We will need a doctor and a teacher for Nala. Send us good recruits; we need *men.* Where will the funds come from? They will come from God. Nala is a magnificent station, a golden opportunity." C.T. addressed the letter to Martin Sutton, chairman of the board, and waited for the Belgian mail boat to arrive.

When the mail boat did arrive, C.T. exchanged the letters he had written for letters from home. He was shocked when he opened one of the letters from Priscilla. Both Martin Sutton and his loyal supporter Lord Radstock had died within a year of each other.

C.T. was so used to setbacks by now that he knew he would keep going, even though the mission board was now stacked against him. He wrote to his new friend Count de Grunne and asked for a concession of land in Nala. He received a prompt reply offering him land, as long as the local people agreed to having missionaries in their midst. This meant a second trip to Nala, and C.T. and Alfred left as soon as they could. When they reached Nala, they rode their bicycles into town. The local people cheered excitedly and gathered around them, glad to see that the missionaries had returned.

C.T. and Alfred stayed several days in Nala, and before they left, the head men put their thumbprints on an official paper to signify that a lovely tract of land in their village would belong to the Heart of Africa Mission. As C.T. looked at the land, he could already picture a thriving school and a hospital on the site.

Before C.T. and Alfred left Nala, a man named Sambo had become a Christian. C.T. hoped that Sambo would be the first of many believers in Nala.

To further encourage C.T.'s faith, a letter soon arrived from the mission board. Much to C.T.'s surprise, it stated that the board had dispatched five more missionaries to join them. C.T. was overjoyed.

Three months later C.T. and Alfred made two more long treks, one to Poko, five days northwest of Nala, and another six days farther on to Bambili. C.T. considered both of these sites ideal for mission stations, and he wrote to Count de Grunne applying for land concessions at both places.

C.T. felt as if things were breaking open at last. Since arriving in the Congo, he and Alfred had found four strategic centers for mission stations, and the work from these stations could easily reach eight different tribes. But hundreds of workers were needed in the Congo, not just five! So while still in Bambili, C.T. and Alfred decided on a plan to expand the work further. Alfred was to go back to Niangara and meet up with the new missionaries. Together they would start the mission station at Nala. Alfred's job would be to oversee the new station and continue his work writing down the Bangala language.

Meanwhile C.T. would venture on another three hundred miles to meet up with the Congo River. He would then canoe seven hundred miles downstream to the river's mouth. From there he would take a ship back to England to enlist more recruits. He knew that this would be made more difficult because a war had broken out in Europe, pitting Germany against Russia, France, and Great Britain. Young men were being recruited for service in the trenches in France. But C.T. was sure that he could make a good case for Christian men to consider volunteering for the noble task of fighting for the souls of men in the Congo.

In February 1915 C.T. and Alfred went their separate ways. The two missionaries had been together for two years. In that time C.T. had watched Alfred grow from a spindly twenty-year-old into a mature man. As they parted company, C.T. prayed that this maturity would be enough to sustain Alfred until he could arrive back from England with more help. Neither man had any idea how long that would be.

Chapter 13

Bwana Mukubwa

By April C.T. was back in England. On one hand, he was delighted to see his wife and daughters again and hold his first grandchild, but in other ways he found being in his homeland very difficult. He sat in overstuffed chairs in dining rooms, drinking out of china cups and eating dainty cakes and chocolates, and he did not like it one bit. The humor he once possessed was gone, and everything he saw was influenced by his recent hardships and the needs he had witnessed in the Congo. C.T. scrutinized every "frivolity" and even some things most people would argue were necessities. To him, saving a halfpenny here and a sixpence there meant more funds to open another mission station.

The Great War raging in Europe brought into sharp focus the urgency C.T. felt about the fight for souls. C.T. used the war to spur Christian volunteers for Africa. In one of the first articles he wrote for the Heart of Africa Mission newsletter after arriving home, he said,

> There are more than twice as many Christian uniformed officers at home among peaceful Britain's 40 million evangelized inhabitants than the whole number of Christ's forces fighting at the front among 1,200 million heathen! And yet such call themselves soldiers of Christ! What do the angels call them, I wonder. The "Let's-save-Britain-first" brigade are in the succession of the "I-pray-thee-have-me-excused" apostles.
>
> Christ's call is to feed the hungry, not the full; to save the lost, not the stiff-necked; not to call the scoffers, but sinners to repentance; not to build and furnish comfortable chapels, churches, and cathedrals at home in which to rock Christian professors to sleep by means of clever essays, stereotyped prayer and artistic musical performances, but to raise living churches of souls among the destitute, to capture men from the devil's clutches and snatch them from the very jaws of hell, to enlist and train them for Jesus, and make them into an almighty Army of God. But this can only be accomplished by a red-hot, unconventional,

> unfettered Holy Ghost religion, where neither Church nor State, neither man nor traditions are worshiped or preached, but only Christ and Him crucified. Not to confess Christ by fancy collars, clothes, silver croziers or gold watch-chain crosses, church steeples or richly embroidered altar cloths, but by reckless sacrifice and heroism in the foremost trenches.

This and other similar articles made C.T. a lightning rod for controversy everywhere he went. Some Christians welcomed him with open arms, urging him to shake up the church even more, while others bristled at his abrasive message. C.T. did not care. He went up and down the country preaching and urging Christians to be wholehearted for God and to be as willing to fight for the gospel in foreign lands as they were willing to fight for England in the Great War.

All of the traveling took a physical toll on C.T., who still suffered from frequent bouts of malaria. But C.T. went on traveling and speaking. On November 2, 1915, he wrote in his diary.

> Hughes Jones, my host, brought in a doctor, who forbade me to go out and speak that evening and said that I must go home at once. I laughed and spoke for an hour and a half; [the] next day at Carnarvon, two hours; then Bangor, three meetings; and then

> Aberystwyth. Oh, these train journeys! So slow and cold, but God is always there.

C.T. refused to spare himself in the cause of bringing the gospel to Central Africa. In another article he wrote of his vision for the Heart of Africa Mission to be the first of many missions to unreached tribes. He ended the article by saying, "Worldwide it is! Thank God I don't know how to retreat!"

Letters from Alfred Buxton were for the most part encouraging. Although one of the newly arrived missionaries had died from a tropical disease, the rest were "on fire," as Alfred put it, and getting results. Six months after C.T. had left the Congo for England, Alfred reported that eighteen people had been baptized. He wrote, "Each of these Nala baptisms would make stirring headlines, 'Ex-cannibals, Drunkards, Thieves, Murderers, Adulterers, and Swearers enter the Kingdom of God.'"

C.T. was thrilled as he read more of Alfred's account of what was happening at Nala.

> At the meeting for the confession of sin, we had some remarkable testimonies: "I have done more sin than there is room for in my chest." "My father killed a man, and I helped to eat him." "I did witchcraft from the finger nails of a dead man, and with the medicine killed a man." Each [person] is greeted, when they first come, with "What have you come here for? Because I tell you frankly

> there is not much money to be got here; our men have enough to live on, but all we really care about is getting men to learn about God and to read His Word." In spite of such a greeting, one and all have answered, "We do not care a snap about money, what we want is God."

Finally, by June 1916, C.T. had gathered eight recruits to take back with him to the Congo. Among them were his daughter Edith, who planned to marry Alfred, a female pharmacist, and a carpenter. It had taken months to get the money together for their passages to Africa, and just as they were ready to leave, C.T. received bad news. George Buxton, Alfred's older brother, who had been planning to join Alfred in the Congo, had instead been conscripted into the British army as a pilot. George's biplane was shot down flying over enemy lines one day, and George was killed.

Saddened by the news, C.T. continued to prepare for the group's departure. In July everything was ready, and C.T. nailed posters up around London.

> All day prayer and praise, 10:00 AM to 10:00 PM, Central Hall, Westminster. Inauguration of Christ's Crusade by the farewelling of Mr. C.T. Studd and party for the Heart of Africa. Your prayers are earnestly invited for the outgoing party leaving Paddington on Monday 24th, at 9:40. Confetti would be out

> of place, but a shower-bath of Hallelujahs is always in season.

And hallelujahs there were as C.T. preached to an enthusiastic crowd that day. C.T. thundered from the pulpit, "Christ wants not nibblers of the possible but grabbers of the impossible. Some wish to live within the sound of church or chapel bells. I want to run a rescue shop within a yard of hell!"

A huge crowd gathered at Paddington Station on July 24, 1916, to see the band of missionaries off. Priscilla was there, this time saying farewell to not only her husband but also her daughter. As at other times, C.T. and Priscilla had said their good-byes privately before going to the station. Finally, with a hiss of smoke from the train's engine, C.T. Studd was once again on his way back to Africa.

The sea voyage from England held extra dangers this time. German U-boats were prowling the Atlantic Ocean, torpedoing British ships. All of the portholes in the ship the missionaries traveled on were blacked out, and a constant watch was kept for the enemy. Because of the tense situation, no idle sightseers were on this ship, only the missionaries and a large contingent of Belgian officials being sent to man postes in the Congo. Some of the Belgians mocked C.T. and his eight missionary recruits, but C.T. did not care. As usual, opposition only served to focus his thoughts and spur him on.

Besides, C.T. had more important things to consider than the taunts of the Belgian officials or

German U-boats. In his care were eight idealistic young people, none of whom, with the exception of Edith, had ever before been out of England. C.T. did all he could to prepare them for the primitive conditions that lay ahead. But even as he did so, he wondered how much of it they were able to comprehend. Could they even imagine a world where there was no running water, no familiar food, and no privacy? He called his "troops" together every morning to study the Bangala language and each afternoon to study great heroes of the faith from the Bible. They spent their evenings praying for what lay ahead.

They encountered no German U-boats on their voyage, and finally, on September 27, 1916, the ship sailed into the mouth of the Congo River and docked at Matadi. The missionaries camped there for five days while they gathered supplies and waited for a train to take them on a twelve-hour journey to Kinshasa. The long, jarring train ride was followed by a voyage on a steamer two hundred miles up the Congo River. There was no wind, and it was stiflingly hot, but C.T. continued to drill his troops every day. When the steamer docked at the confluence of the Congo and the Welle rivers, Alfred was waiting to greet them.

A few awkward moments followed as Alfred and Edith got reacquainted, but by evening Edith was beaming. After three and a half years apart, Alfred was still the man she remembered and wanted to marry.

Before setting out on the next leg of their journey, Alfred caught C.T. up on all that had happened in his absence. The stories Alfred told warmed C.T.'s heart. There were now sixty baptized Christians in Nala, and many of the chiefs from the surrounding areas were requesting that missionaries come to their villages.

"I won't deny that we've done a lot of work," Alfred said, "but we have also seen God working miracles. One of our missionaries came across a tribe who asked him if he was English. When he told them he was, they brought him to a man who recounted the most astonishing story. Several years before, when he was a teenager, this man had a vivid dream. In the dream God told him, 'Wait for the English; they will tell you about Me.' Ever since, the people of the village had questioned any white person who crossed their path, asking if he was English. They did not know that English was a nationality and assumed it meant a god-person. Our missionary was able to set them straight and introduce them to Jesus Christ."

C.T. smiled. "God still works by giving dreams, just as he did to Daniel. If every conversion in Britain is a miracle, any conversion in Africa is a thousand times greater miracle!"

The group boarded a smaller steamer for the one-week journey up the Welle River before they set out on foot for the last three hundred miles of the journey. By the time they neared Nala, they had been traveling for four months and were all exhausted. C.T. had battled his familiar bouts with malaria, though he preferred to think of them as bouts with the devil from which he emerged the winner every time.

The group was still several days' trek from Nala when it began to encounter groups of African Christians along the track. These Africans marched beside them singing hymns and reciting Bible passages. More than once, tears sprang to C.T.'s eyes as the enormity of it all sank in. In the two years he had been away, Christianity had taken root in one of the darkest places he knew of.

Finally C.T. informed his weary band of missionaries that they were within a half day's walk of their destination. Their spirits rose and their pace quickened at the thought. By noon they were at the outskirts of the village. Cries of joy went up from the Christians as they rushed out to greet C.T. and the new missionaries. One of the first to greet them was Sambo, the first convert from Nala. Sambo had waited nearly two years for C.T. to return.

C.T. laughed with delight when he saw Sambo. Sambo had with him three friends, and between them they balanced a long native drum on their heads. Propped on top of the drum was a four-year-old boy, who beat the drum with a stick. Sambo told C.T. that he wanted to welcome him back in style!

The people of Nala had prepared a tropical feast for C.T. and his companions. Pineapples and bananas adorned roughhewn tables, and roast chicken, sweet potatoes, and greens soon emerged from ovens and were placed on the tables.

As they ate, C.T. eagerly questioned the remaining four missionaries who had arrived soon after his departure for England. He was keen to learn what each one had been doing while he was away.

When the meal was over, C.T. sat back and surveyed the scene. The last time he had been in Nala, it consisted of a few abandoned buildings surrounded by huts and an avenue of palm trees. Now it was a thriving village, the Christian center of the region. It had many new houses, including small ones for each of the new missionaries.

That night the regular Friday evening service was held in a huge, open-sided meetinghouse. C.T. watched in awe as two hundred Africans quietly took their places on wooden benches. The peoples well-oiled bodies gleamed in the lamplight, and their faces shined. C.T. thought he had never heard anything more beautiful than the hymns they sang that night. The hymns were Bangala hymns that Alfred had made up and taught to the people while C.T. was away. One hymn, which they sang with particular gusto, went like this:

The road to hell is broad,
The devil keeps it well swept.
Very many people travel on it,
Because madness has seized them.

The road to heaven is difficult,
There is a stream to cross.
But there is only one canoe to ferry you over,
The name of the canoe is Jesus.

Following the hymns came a time for sharing testimonies, and there were many testimonies to tell. C.T. was humbled by the faith evident in them. One man, who had a sore on his leg, stood and said, "I have walked many a mile through the forests on these legs to do my own will. Now I have given myself to God. I only wait for my wound to heal, and I shall use them to preach the gospel."

Another man then rose to his feet. He had no ears. "I am Miyeye, and many people ask me what happened to my ears," he began in a high-pitched voice. "The truth is I have eaten them. Many years ago I was a slave in a chief's village. My life was very difficult. I worked harder than most, but I was paid less, and I was often hungry. One day I happened to talk to one of the chief's wives, who was also being treated badly, and we decided to run away together. As soon as it got dark, we ran and ran. But we were not fast. I was a boy and she was a woman, and soon the chief's men caught up to us. They dragged us back to the village, and a big fire was lit under a pot. Before my eyes the wife was killed and cooked, but when it came my turn, the chief's head wife ran through the crowd: 'We must not cook the child. It will bring a curse on us all if we eat a child, and we shall die.'

"The chief stared at me for a long time and then nodded. 'As you say, we shall not cook him, but he must be punished. Chop off his ears, cook them, and make him eat them.' And that is what they did. It was terrible, and I was sick for many days. But now, all these years later, I have heard of the God who forgives me and asks me to forgive others, and I have forgiven the chief. My heart dances with joy."

Tears streamed down C.T.'s face as he listened. He wished that all the skeptical Christians in England could sit right where he was and listen to testimonies like these. There was no doubt in his mind that the power of God was at work in the dark jungles around them.

Three weeks later C.T. was on the move again. It was time for a wedding, and so they made their way to Niangara, where the new Belgian district commissioner and the district judge lived. Count de Grunne, the old district commissioner who had been so helpful to C.T. when he first arrived in the region, had died of blackwater fever several months before.

Edith's arrival in Niangara caused quite a stir, because she and the other two women in the group were the only white women in the Congo. The Belgian government had not permitted any other women, including the wives of their officials, to travel to the country. The government maintained that the Congo was not civilized enough for women.

Because of this, Edith and Alfred's wedding was the first white wedding to be held in the heart of the

Congo. Two days after Christmas 1916, the wedding took place in two stages. The first stage was a church service held in the little mission station built by C.T. and Alfred and previously named Buckingham Palace. Stepping inside the mud building brought back many memories to C.T. The locals, both Christians and non-Christians, crowded in to watch the spectacle. About halfway through the service, an overloaded bench snapped in half, and thirty Africans fell to the floor. Once it was established that no one was hurt, the service continued. Later that day, ten Belgian officials gathered with the missionaries to witness the district commissioner carry out the legal ceremony. The officials were all arrayed in their white dress uniforms, replete with medals, for the historic occasion. Tea and wedding cake followed.

Alfred and Edith honeymooned on a nearby island while C.T. returned to Nala, now the headquarters of the mission. The locals there soon dubbed C.T. Bwana Mukubwa—Great White Chief.

Chapter 14

God Is to Be Found in Nala

In front of C.T. stood eighty-one Africans, all waiting to be baptized. C.T. had spoken to each one personally, listening to his or her testimony and questioning his or her understanding of the Bible. Some candidates were old, others young. Many were humble jungle dwellers, while three of them were important chiefs. This made C.T. very happy. C.T. believed that their willingness to be baptized at the same time spoke volumes about their understanding of being brothers and sisters in Christ. He was satisfied that they all understood the step they were taking. Now, as hymn after hymn was sung, each candidate waded into a pool in the river and was baptized. It reminded C.T. of the time twelve years before when he had baptized all four of his daughters in India.

Within a week of being baptized, several people told C.T. that they were now ready to go out and preach the gospel to their tribes and even to tribes farther away. C.T. was delighted and called a meeting for all those who felt led to become missionaries. About twenty people, their faces shining, showed up for the meeting. Sambo, the first convert at Nala, was among their number.

This was more than C.T. had hoped for, and he became very excited about the amount of work that so many on-fire Christians could accomplish. Soon the details were worked out. Each native missionary would be paid three francs and be expected to stay away for three months. The money would be enough to cover the cost of food if the missionary was careful. Each man or woman would travel light, carrying a grass mat for a bed and a second one for a blanket. Each would also take with him or her a jungle knife and an enamel cup.

A month later C.T. gathered the twenty new missionaries together under a mango tree. This was their last meeting, and C.T. had some advice for them. He wiped his brow and began.

"This is my final advice to you, so listen carefully. One. If you don't desire to meet the devil during the day, meet Jesus before dawn. Two. If you don't want the devil to hit you, hit him first and with all your might so that he may be too crippled to hit back. 'Preach the Word' is the rod the devil fears and hates. Three. If you don't want to fall, walk, and walk straight and fast. Four. Three of the devil's dogs with which he hunts us are a swelled head, laziness, and cupidity. Now, I want to pray for you all, as you know I will continue to do each day you are gone."

After the prayer several of the missionaries rushed up to C.T. One of them asked, "How long are we to stay out in the jungle?"

"If you are tired, return at the end of one month. If you are not, return at the end of two, and if you can stick it out for three, well done!" C.T. replied.

"Oh, no!" one man exclaimed. "I won't be back for a year."

"Then I'm not coming back for eighteen months," a second man responded.

C.T. smiled at their enthusiasm. He visited as many of the native missionaries as he could during the following weeks, and he marveled at the sacrifices they were making and the results they were reaping. He seldom stopped to think that they were merely following his example.

Sambo, who encountered a lot of opposition from a local chief, reported to C.T., "There is nothing outside that can take away the joy inside."

On April 14, 1917, C.T. sat down at his folding table and began to write.

> The work here is a marvel, quite beyond my conception; the finger of God is writ all over it. We arrived here two strangers three and a half years ago, the natives sunk in sin unprintable, the medium of communications to be

> learned, yet there are just upon 100 baptized converts. Many Chiefs are beginning to build schools and other houses at their centers, that we may go and instruct their people. Everywhere we have an open door for ourselves and our native Christians.

As the native missionaries returned to Nala, many of them put their entire three months' pay back into the offering. They had not spent a penny of it. Their stories inspired many others, and by August fifty more people wanted to be baptized, and many of them wanted to go out as missionaries as well. C.T., Alfred, and the others all labored to prepare them for the task.

As the church grew, people begged to be taught how to read the Bible, and two schools, one for boys and one for girls, were started.

By May 1918, one year later, people were streaming into Nala from the outlying villages. Amazingly, as word spread, some came from even farther afield. A group of four men walked for twenty days to get to Nala. When they arrived, they told C.T., "We have come because all the world knows that the knowledge of God is to be found in Nala."

Baptisms were now being held every Sunday, and chiefs came to Nala in person to ask for missionaries to come to their villages. Some of them announced that they had already built a chapel and a mission house for their missionary!

The following month C.T. went on one of his bicycle tours, which took him to the village of Deti in Ituri province. C.T. explained the gospel to the chief and his head wife. The chief's wife understood it instantly and became very excited. "I always said there should be a god like that!" she exclaimed.

Soon the chief had heard enough to offer C.T. a plot of land if someone would come and teach his village. C.T. decided it was too good an opportunity to pass up, and so when he returned to Nala, he dispatched the Ellises, a married couple, to set up a mission station in Deti.

Six months later C.T. returned to Deti to see the progress the Ellises had made. What he saw astonished him. One of the first converts was a blind man named Ndabani. When Ndabani was a teenager, someone had rubbed hot peppers in his eyes to prevent him from ever becoming chief. Now he was a chief among the growing number of Christians in Deti.

On Sunday morning C.T. watched as people began to arrive soon after dawn for the weekly worship service. By the time the service began, the meetinghouse was so tightly packed that C.T. had difficulty weaving his way through the crowd to get to the pulpit.

From the pulpit C.T. preached a sermon that was translated into the local Kingwana language. Even though an interpreter had to be used, the local people sat in rapt silence, their eyes fastened on C.T.

At the end of the meeting, C.T. prayed that the Deti church would soon be sending out missionaries of its own.

From Deti C.T. hurried back to Nala. A special event was about to take place. C.T.'s daughter Edith was about to give birth—to the first white child born in the Congo. C.T. arrived in Nala just in time for his granddaughter Susan's arrival. Soon after, a special prayer meeting was held to thank God for the safe delivery of the child.

Prayer meetings were also held for other reasons. One of the most frequent reasons was the need for staff for the school. Since none of the adults in the village had ever been to school themselves, they could not read or write and so could not be trained as schoolteachers. And because of the war in Europe, no new missionary recruits had arrived in over a year and a half.

Sometimes workers appeared from the most unlikely places. One day a man, his wife, and a porter arrived at Nala. The man introduced himself as Gamutu from the Asande tribe. He got straight to the point. "Bwana," he said to C.T., "I have walked two hundred miles to come and hear about God. I was in my village when a man came through and told us that at Nala you taught about God. I have always wanted to know about God, so my wife and I packed up at once, and here we are. When is the first lesson?"

C.T. laughed with joy at Gamutu's enthusiasm. It wasn't long before his laughter turned to deep admiration as he became aware of Gamutu's natural leadership ability and his quick mind. Within a year Gamutu had risen to the position of head of the boys' school.

It was a good thing that the native people were taking on positions of responsibility in the church and the school, because the time had come for Alfred and Edith to take a furlough. Alfred had been living in the Congo for five years by now, and it was time for a break. C.T. hoped that while Alfred was away in England, he would stir up interest in the work in the Congo and bring back a fresh group of recruits with him.

On the morning that Alfred, Edith, and baby Susan were due to leave, a huge meeting was held in the church. Hundreds of people came to say goodbye to them. C.T. spoke briefly at the service.

"Alfred has been to me as a loyal son and heart companion," he began. "None but God can ever know the deep and spiritual communion, for no words can describe it. To Alfred's nursing and care, under God, I certainly owe my life."

When C.T. finished speaking, Alfred asked for him to lay hands on his head and offer a last prayer.

C.T. walked over to Alfred and said, "I will pray only if you do as I ask you. Stand on your chair."

Obediently, but a little bewildered, Alfred climbed up onto his chair. Then C.T. stooped down and laid his hands on Alfred's feet. Tears fell freely as he prayed that God would keep Alfred, Edith, and Susan safe and bring them home to Nala.

C.T. was surprised how lonely he felt without Alfred by his side, but good news soon cheered him up. The Great War was finally over, and Priscilla wrote, promising to send more missionaries by early 1920. Among the new missionaries who arrived was C.T.'s daughter Pauline and her husband, Norman Grubb.

It was as if a fresh wind were blowing in England, and Priscilla's letters were filled with optimism and hope. Gilbert Barclay, Dorothy's husband, was now chairman of the board of the Heart of Africa Mission. C.T. was delighted, especially because Gilbert had the same vision to see H.A.M. expanded around the world. In keeping with this goal, Gilbert lobbied to have H.A.M.'s name changed to Worldwide Evangelism Crusade, or WEC for short.

Letters followed, detailing plans for making WEC an international organization. The organization purchased the house at number 19 Highland Road to serve as an overflow for the missionary guests who now streamed through the Studd house. Then, later in 1920 Priscilla and Alfred went on a tour of the United States to recruit missionaries and rally financial support for the work in the Congo and the new work in the Amazon Basin in South America that WEC planned to start.

Edith stayed behind in London while her mother and Alfred were in the United States. And in London she gave birth to a second child, a son they named Lionel.

There was other news too. Priscilla decided that C.T. needed a secretary and announced that a Miss May Wilson had been dispatched to the Congo. Miss Wilson was bringing with her a supply of paper and her own typewriter. C.T. was not sure whether he liked this idea. Up until now he had been handling his own correspondence, though in a quiet moment he did have to admit that at sixty years of age it was getting a little much for him.

While he was somewhat indifferent about the arrival of Miss Wilson, C.T. looked forward to Alfred's return. He had no idea of the great struggle that lay ahead for both of them.

Chapter 15

A New Venture

"Welcome back!" C.T. said as he gave Alfred a hearty slap on the back. He turned to Edith and hugged her. "God understands your sacrifice," he whispered in her ear. He was referring to the fact that Edith had left both of her children, two-and-a-half-year-old Susan and baby Lionel, back in England with her mother-in-law. Both children had chest complaints, and doctors had warned Alfred and Edith that it would endanger their lives for them to return to the Congo with their parents.

It was early 1921, though C.T. had all but forgotten the importance of European time. He had been living in the Congo for five years now without a break, and he did not want one. "No," he told anyone who asked. "God told me to come to the Congo, and I'm not leaving until He tells me to!"

By now C.T. walked with a stoop, and all of his teeth were either broken or missing completely. "Don't you want to go home and get a new set of teeth made?" people would ask him.

"If God wants me to have some new teeth, He can just as easily send someone to me as send me to them!" C.T. would reply.

His fellow missionaries laughed at this and remonstrated him for being impossible, but C.T. did not care.

Now that Alfred and Edith were back in Nala, C.T. thought about moving to another location. He had made several preaching trips south to Ibambi, and he was impressed with the amazing number of new believers in the area. After praying about it, C.T. felt that God was directing him to move there.

Word that Bwana Mukubwa was on his way to Ibambi spread quickly, and hundreds of Christians gathered to sing hymns for C.T. as he walked through their territory. C.T. was overwhelmed by the gesture.

Once in Ibambi, it did not take C.T. long to set up house. He still used the same folding chair and cot that he had brought to the jungle with him. On his second day in Ibambi, he began learning Kingwana, the local language. And just as in Nala, Ibambi soon became a hub of Christian activity in the area.

Five hours' walk beyond Ibambi lay the village of Chief Imbai. The residents of this village had constructed a church that seated 1,250 people. The church was known as the "cricket pitch church," because it was the length of a cricket pitch. Sometimes when C.T. stood at the front of this church, he thought of his cricketing days. Staring down the long building, he imagined he was up to bat, his eyes focused on the bowler at the other end of the pitch. But his cricket days seemed far off to him now—a lifetime away, in fact. What mattered to C.T. now were not the cheers of the spectators or the opinion of sports commentators but the souls of those around him.

Always C.T. looked for signs that the African converts—men, women, and children—understood the gospel and that their lives were truly changed by it. He saw many such signs. In fact, Chief Imbai was a case in point. He had been called before the Belgian officials and told, "You are entitled to ask six hundred francs a year in rent for the church Bwana Mukubwa uses. We will write up the documents and help you collect the money."

"Oh, no!" Chief Imbai replied. "I have given that land to God, and I cannot take any money for it now."

The Belgian officials could not believe what the chief was saying, and so they repeated the offer three times. Each time they got the same answer, until they came to accept the fact that Chief Imbai refused to take any of the payment to which he was entitled.

At another village, three hours' walk from Ibambi, six hundred Africans met every Sunday for worship. Many of them brought mats with them so they could sleep the night in the church and continue the service on Monday.

Wherever C.T. was, he preached and read the Bible aloud. Often, when he stopped, the people sent up howls of protest. "Don't stop now," the old men and women would yell. "We have not heard these words before, and we may die before we hear them again, so keep reading to us."

In all his forty years as a missionary, C.T. had never seen such openness to the gospel. More native missionaries than ever before were going out to witness to other tribes, and the stories they told were amazing. One missionary was beaten for witnessing in a village, and when the beating was over, he got up, shook the chief's hand, and thanked him for the honor of being beaten for Jesus. Another missionary was put in jail, and within a few hours many of his new converts crowded around the jail, asking for the privilege of being locked up along with their brother.

These stories and many others like them convinced C.T. that he was in the right place. Although the mission board at home and his two sons-in-law in the Congo tried to persuade him that he needed to go home for a break, C.T. would not hear of it. He wrote to the board, trying his best to explain himself.

> And do you think that I can consent to turn a deaf ear to the cries of these people clamoring for the gospel and craving for teachers? If I can't send them teachers because there are

> no teachers to send, yet at least I can stop one yawning gap myself. If I am not so efficient as youngsters, yet at least I may be more efficient than an absentee, a nobody. And if others have failed to hear and respond to these awful pleadings of sinful men going to hell, yet desiring to know the way to heaven, at least my presence can assure them that there is still some who to save them will count life and all they hold dear as of no account in comparison.

Bouts of malaria continued to plague C.T. at regular intervals. One night, soon after he had settled in at Ibambi, he was so ill that Alfred and Edith came to take care of him. They brought news that Pauline had given birth to a healthy boy, whom she and Norman named Noel. Alfred bathed C.T. and sat with him until midnight and then returned to the adjoining hut to get some rest.

About two hours later C.T. was awakened by a piercing scream. It was Edith. Moments later she dashed into C.T.'s hut. "Father, it's Alfred," she gasped. "He started convulsing, and now he's not moving."

C.T. willed himself to get up from his cot, and leaning on Edith for support, he shuffled over to examine his son-in-law. Alfred lay in bed under his mosquito net, breathing lightly. C.T.'s shaking hands ran over Alfred's neck and chest and down to his wrist to take his pulse.

"This must be some kind of fit," C.T. told his daughter.

C.T. sat propped up beside Alfred the rest of the night, though it would have been difficult for anyone looking in to say who was the nurse and who was the patient. By morning Alfred was conscious again, though he was weak and disoriented. It was weeks before he was able to take up his normal workload again.

By now forty missionaries were working in the Congo with WEC, and letters arrived from Priscilla saying that WEC had finally expanded its work into the Amazon, sending three missionaries there as an advance team. And thanks to Priscilla and Alfred's visit to the United States the year before, an American arm of WEC had been established. Now WEC U.S.A. was promising to send missionaries to the Congo within the year.

As for the missionaries already serving with C.T., many of them were courageous and self-sacrificing. However, inevitably some began to question the austere life C.T. asked them to lead. They asked what was wrong with having a day off or a wooden table and chairs and glass windows in their huts, and even food supplies from home so they could enjoy a Western meal once in a while.

C.T. hardly knew how to respond to these "soft" missionaries. As in the past, he found his outlet in pouring out his feelings in his journal.

> While here in the saddle I intend to ride and get others to ride, and not be carried to

> heaven on a flowery bed of ease. Let us do one thing or the other—either eat and drink, for tomorrow we die, or let us gamble with life and death and all for our Lord Jesus. None but gamblers wanted out here; let the grumblers go home.

Several months later, news came that Noel Grubb, Pauline and Norman's son, had died suddenly on his first birthday. C.T. grieved for his daughter and son-in-law, remembering the two sons he had buried, but he continued to bury himself in the work around him. He spent his weekdays teaching and translating in the Kingwana language and his weekends evangelizing in the outlying areas.

C.T. liked to start his weekend trips at seven o'clock on Friday night. That meant he could work all day Friday and then, when it got dark, set off for his destination. In his younger days, he had walked or bicycled everywhere he went, but now he allowed eight strong men to carry him in a canvas pole-chair. Those carrying him were committed Christians. Otherwise they could never have been induced to venture out at night into leopard-infested jungles. C.T. hated being treated as someone important, but he had to concede that he was too weak to get far on his own.

C.T. took very little with him on his trips, just a few blankets, a lamp, some medicines to give out along the way, and his Bible. He would climb into the pole-chair, which would then be gently lifted onto the willing shoulders of his carriers. The leader would carry a spear and a lantern and head off into the night. C.T. would normally order a halt around midnight and settle down to rest until daylight. Then the party would carry him on the last few miles to their destination. Meanwhile, the natives along the way beat news of Bwana Mukubwa's arrival, and hundreds of people would start out to meet C.T.

When he arrived at a mission station, C.T. would have a cup of tea and talk to the missionaries about what was going on in the local area. Then he would lie down for a while to gather strength for a big midday service. C.T. was always awed by the number of people who straggled in to hear him speak. It was not unusual for over two thousand people, prompted by the drums, to gather for a service, where they would sing hymns, pray, and listen to a sermon. At night a large, fallen tree limb would often be set alight to warm anyone who wanted to stay overnight. Most people did stay, and sometimes they'd stay the night after that. It was not unusual for C.T. to have to announce on a Wednesday morning that he had to get back to his other work and say goodbye to the gathered crowd.

It was a grueling schedule, but one that C.T. drove himself to keep. C.T. felt that not a minute was to be wasted!

In the rainy season of 1921, two sets of people came to Ibambi. The first comprised an Englishman and his three porters. The man strolled into C.T.'s hut one afternoon and greeted C.T. as one would greet an old friend.

"My name is John Buck. I have come a long way to meet you, sir," he said.

"Well, drink tea with me and tell me who you are," C.T. replied.

"I suppose I should start at the beginning," the visitor said as he sank into one of C.T.'s spare folding chairs. "I am a dentist, and a year and a half ago God told me to go to the Congo and fix your teeth. I applied to WEC to be a dentist missionary, but they rejected me because I was too old."

C.T. studied John Buck's face, and, concluding that John must be only half his own age, he laughed.

"Anyway, I still had my heavenly orders to fix your teeth, so I gave up my business in London and sailed for Africa. I would have been here sooner, but I took six months' work in Nairobi to earn the money for the rest of the journey. So here I am."

For once in his life, C.T. was speechless. God had actually sent a dentist halfway around the world to fix his teeth!

Over the next week John extracted C.T.'s remaining teeth and molded a set of false teeth for him. C.T. was delighted. He could sing much better with his new teeth, and he often used them to play jokes on the local people, none of whom imagined that such a thing as false teeth existed. One time he put a pair of pliers in his mouth and pretended to extract all his top teeth at once. Another time he took his teeth out in the middle of a prayer, leaving those praying with him to wonder how the teeth had all magically disappeared.

The second set of people to come to the Congo—the seven new American missionary recruits from WEC U.S.A.—caused a lot of problems. Alfred was delighted to see them, some of whom he had personally recruited and recommended. But C.T. was not so impressed. All of the missionaries until now had been from Great Britain, and they all belonged to denominations such as the Methodists and Presbyterians. In contrast, the American arrivals were mainly Baptists, and it was not long before the British and American missionaries were arguing bitterly over different interpretations of certain Bible verses. Instead of helping to soothe the quarreling, C.T. joined in on the side of the British missionaries. Within weeks the American WEC missionaries announced that they would not be part of the mission and marched out of camp, never to return.

At first everyone was stunned, and then accusations started to fly. Alfred was particularly horrified that the Americans had met with such hostility from the British missionaries. He questioned C.T.'s judgment in involving himself in the debate rather than quelling it.

Worse was to follow. The American WEC missionaries wrote back to their home base, and soon WEC U.S.A. was threatening to withdraw its support and become an independent organization.

Other issues began to create tension between C.T. and Alfred. One was that despite the fact that Priscilla was now traveling the world representing WEC, C.T. forbade her to come and visit him in the

Congo. Officially he cited the fact that Priscilla was too important a person in the mission to run the risk of catching tropical diseases, but something deeper pulled at his heart. C.T. would not go home unless God told him to, and he was afraid that if Priscilla came to visit him, he would not be able to help himself from wanting her to stay at his side. This would mean that either he had to return to England or she would have to stop her effective recruiting campaign and join him permanently. As an old soldier who had put his mission first for nearly fifty years, he could not allow either of those options to occur. So C.T. concluded that it would be better if they did not see each other again.

As the 1920s progressed, the letters C.T. received from the board of WEC began more and more to question his decisions. C.T. decided that he needed to send Pauline and Norman home to explain the situation in person. Before they left, Pauline came to say good-bye to her father. C.T. had a strange feeling he would never see his daughter again, and he looked around his room for something of value to give her. His eyes scanned an old Nestlé milk can with some pencils in it, a couple of well-worn Bibles, his comb, and a patched set of clothes. Seeing nothing else, he shook his head and said, "Pauline, I would really like to give you something, but I find that I gave everything I had to Jesus years ago."

Chapter 16

No Chocolate Soldier

A great feeling of relief surged over C.T. It was July 1926, and C.T. had lived long enough to finish translating the New Testament and Psalms into the Kingwana language. He checked the translation one last time and then packaged it up and sent it off by mail to the coast to be published. So many things, including the mail, were easier now. In times past, a runner had to make a twelve-hour journey from Nala to rendezvous with the nearest mail service. Now roads had branched out into the Congo, and one came all the way to Ibambi. A mail car now came there once a week bringing packages and letters.

One letter the mail car brought was from Alfred Buxton. In the letter Alfred explained that he and

Edith were in the United States. They had been invited there to discuss the future of WEC U.S.A. and in particular why the first set of WEC missionaries had been so poorly welcomed. C.T. was outraged by this news. He felt that the fault lay entirely at the feet of the American missionaries and that the work had been hurt by their disagreement and departure. He fumed at the idea that Alfred and Edith were trying to smooth things over. Before he had time to let his feelings subside and get a clear picture of the situation, C.T. shot back a letter to Alfred. In it he told Alfred that he was being disloyal and that he could consider himself dismissed from the mission. Edith, his own daughter, need not come back either. Regrettably C.T. could not see beyond his personal feelings in this matter.

The missionaries serving in the Congo were shocked when they heard what C.T. had done. Alfred had helped establish the Heart of Africa Mission in the Congo and had been a loyal part of it for thirteen years.

In February 1928 the mail car brought a different cargo to Ibambi. When it stopped in the village, Priscilla Studd stepped out of it. This time she had not asked C.T. for permission to visit. Instead she had simply informed him when to expect her. C.T., thirty missionaries, and two thousand native Christians were there to meet her. Many of them laughed with delight at seeing "Mama Bwana" for the first time. They had been told many times that C.T. had a wife in England who spent her energies finding more missionaries to send out among them, but many of them seriously doubted that she existed.

Now Priscilla and C.T. stood side by side. Priscilla had given her life serving in England so that the mission would have missionaries and money to carry on its work among the people who now crowded around her. C.T. was amazed at how well she looked at sixty-four years of age, and she was too polite to mention his ancient appearance.

Many difficult things had happened since C.T. and Priscilla had last seen each other, including C.T.'s dismissal of Alfred and Edith. Priscilla told C.T. that Edith was now living in a house in London, while Alfred and some of his American recruits had joined the Sudan Interior Mission and were working in Ethiopia. She also said that as a result of Alfred's dismissal and the persistent rumors that C.T. would not come home for a furlough, even though the mission board demanded he did, many missionaries and supporters had left WEC. Other rumors about C.T.'s being a morphine addict who had lost touch with reality fueled the controversy at home. But these were not matters Priscilla and C.T. discussed at length. It was too painful for them both, and C.T. had no intention of backing down or going "home."

With Mama Bwana in the Congo, a series of daily meetings was hastily arranged at which Priscilla preached through an interpreter. However, Priscilla stayed in the Congo for only two weeks; work back in London called her. This time when the couple parted, C.T. knew for sure that this would be the last time they would see each other on earth. Quietly, in his hut, C.T. said his last farewells to his wife. They prayed together and asked God to bless the work and their children and grandchildren. Then, slowly, arm in arm, they walked down the path to the waiting mail car. The gathered crowd were strangely silent at the sight.

C.T. watched as Priscilla stepped into the car. The door was shut behind her, and she looked straight ahead as she was driven off. C.T. felt that by her doing this, she was saying that they both had tasks to do and would keep their eyes on those tasks with every ounce of strength they had left.

Eleven months later C.T. received a letter from Pauline. After a single day's illness, Priscilla Studd had died on January 29, 1929. C.T.'s last tie to England had been severed, and he knew for a fact that he would never again leave the Congo.

A year later C.T. received word that he had been made a Chevalier of the Royal Order of the Lion by the king of Belgium. He was too weak to go to Kinshasa to collect the award in person, and so it was delivered to him by mail. His native friends were greatly impressed by the medal, but it meant little to C.T. He told everyone that he valued the approval of God far more than the approval of any man, including a king.

In the spring of 1931, C.T. was so ill that he seldom left his bed. However, he still had plenty of company as streams of Christians came to ask him for his blessing and advice. One of them was a little man named Zamu. As he sat beside C.T.'s cot, Zamu explained his reason for visiting. "I have come to say good-bye. I am on my way to the tribes beyond. They are our hereditary enemies, and I wish to bring them the gospel. I have already spoken to Mama Roupell [one of the other missionaries] about it."

"What did she tell you?" C.T. asked.

"She asked me about my foot," Zamu said, looking down at a large ulcer on his left heel. "But I told her, 'God *is,* White Lady.' Then she told me that the food where I was going was very different and that with no palm oil and no salt I might starve. What could I say to her but 'God is, White Lady'? Then she asked me about my wife, and I told her that where I go, my wife will follow. We will walk and talk for God together."

C.T. nodded. He knew Zamu well, and he believed his words.

"Yes, you are right. God is," C.T. replied, pulling up his shirtsleeve. "See this arm of mine, Zamu? Once it was very strong, but now it is weak, and the flesh is shrunken. I cannot go with you; my time is nearly finished among you. I can only go on from day to day as God gives me strength, so don't depend on me; depend on God. He is with you. He won't die. He will keep you."

C.T. then pulled himself up to a sitting position. "Don't go with shame! Don't be afraid! Preach the gospel with boldness. Don't drag the flag of God in the dirt. Hold it high, and don't bring shame upon it. Set your face like a soldier to overcome whatever gets in your way."

Zamu nodded.

"How many of you are going?" C.T. asked.

"Just me and my wife," Zamu replied.

"Ah," C.T. responded, thinking of a time long ago. "That is how I started out, just my wife and I. If you are true, God will make a great company of you one day."

After Zamu left, C.T. lay for a long time thinking back over his life and the decisions he had made. He pulled a piece of paper and his pen and ink off a nearby shelf and wrote in his journal.

> As I believe I am now nearing my departure from this world, I have but a few things to rejoice in; they are these:
>
> 1. That God called me to China and I went in spite of utmost opposition from all my loved ones.
> 2. That I joyfully acted as Christ told that rich young man to act.
> 3. That I deliberately at the call of God, when alone on the Bibby liner [the SS *Warwickshire*] in 1910, gave up my life for this work, which was to be henceforth not for the Sudan only, but for the whole unevangelized world.
>
> My only joys therefore are that when God has given me a work to do, I have not refused it.

By June 1931 C.T. was in great pain. He consulted his medical encyclopedia and decided that he was suffering from a new complaint, gallstones.

For the next month the pain increased daily until he was completely incapacitated. On Thursday, July 16, 1931, C.T. lapsed in and out of consciousness. He fought for every breath he took and often uttered just a single word: "Hallelujah." Soon after dark that day, he died at age seventy.

Twenty years before, when doctors advised C.T. not to go to Africa because he would be dead within weeks, many people asked him what would happen if he did die. C.T. always gave them the same answer. "Shout hallelujah," he would say. "The world will have lost its biggest fool, and with one fool less to handicap Him, God will do greater wonders still. There shall be no funeral, no wreaths, crape, not tears, not even the death march. Congratulations all around will take place. Our God will still be alive, and nothing else matters! To die is gain."

The church at Ibambi decided to follow some but not all of C.T.'s instructions.

"Bwana Mukubwa is dead." The news was carried via beating drums for hundreds of miles in every direction. Soon thousands of people rolled up their sleeping mats, grabbed some green bananas, and started the trek to Ibambi to see C.T.'s body as it lay in an open coffin.

At the sight of his body in the coffin, many people wept, and some touched him one last time or prayed at his feet. A storm hit around noon the next day, but despite the rain and driving wind, over two thousand people watched as C.T.'s coffin was lowered into the muddy African earth. Since no one wanted to leave when the service was over, they held a giant prayer meeting that lasted through the night and into the following day.

When word of C.T.'s death reached London, Alfred Buxton, who despite his dismissal from the mission still held his father-in-law in the highest regard, pulled out an old copy of *The Chocolate Soldier* and read aloud to Edith:

> Every true soldier is a hero! A soldier without heroism is a Chocolate Soldier. Who has not been stirred to scorn and mirth at the very thought of a Chocolate Soldier? In peace true soldiers are captive lions, fretting in their cages. War gives them their liberty and sends them, like boys bounding out of school, to obtain their heart's desire or perish in the attempt. Battle is the soldier's vital breath! Peace turns him into a stooping asthmatic. War makes him a whole man again, and gives him the heart, strength, and vigor of a hero.
>
> Every true Christian is a soldier of Christ, a hero "par excellence"! Braver than the bravest—scorning the soft seductions of peace and her oft repeated warnings against hardship, disease, danger and death, whom he counts among his bosom friends.

Alfred quietly took Edith's hand. "One thing we know for certain," he said softly. "C.T. Studd was no chocolate soldier."

Bibliography

Buxton, Edith. *Reluctant Missionary*. Christian Literature Crusade, 1968.

Erskine, John T. *Millionaire for God: The Story of C.T. Studd*. Christian Literature Crusade, 1968.

Grubb, Norman P. *C.T. Studd: Cricketer and Pioneer*. London: Religious Tract Society, 1934.

Vincent, Eileen. *C.T. Studd and Priscilla*. Eastbourne, England: Kingsway Publications Ltd., 1988.

About the Authors

Janet and Geoff Benge are a husband and wife writing team with more than thirty years of writing experience. Janet is a former elementary school teacher. Geoff holds a degree in history. Originally from New Zealand, the Benges spent ten years serving with Youth With A Mission. They have two daughters, Laura and Shannon, and an adopted son, Lito. They make their home in the Orlando, Florida, area.

Also from Janet and Geoff Benge…

More adventure-filled biographies for ages 10 to 100!

Heroes of History

George Washington Carver: From Slave to Scientist • 978-1-883002-78-7
Abraham Lincoln: A New Birth of Freedom • 978-1-883002-79-4
Meriwether Lewis: Off the Edge of the Map • 978-1-883002-80-0
George Washington: True Patriot • 978-1-883002-81-7
William Penn: Liberty and Justice for All • 978-1-883002-82-4
Harriet Tubman: Freedombound • 978-1-883002-90-9
John Adams: Independence Forever • 978-1-883002-50-3
Clara Barton: Courage under Fire • 978-1-883002-51-0
Daniel Boone: Frontiersman • 978-1-932096-09-5
Theodore Roosevelt: An American Original • 978-1-932096-10-1
Douglas MacArthur: What Greater Honor • 978-1-932096-15-6
Benjamin Franklin: Live Wire • 978-1-932096-14-9
Christopher Columbus: Across the Ocean Sea • 978-1-932096-23-1
Laura Ingalls Wilder: A Storybook Life • 978-1-932096-32-3
Orville Wright: The Flyer • 978-1-932096-34-7
Captain John Smith: A Foothold in the New World • 978-1-932096-36-1
Thomas Edison: Inspiration and Hard Work • 978-1-932096-37-8
Alan Shepard: Higher and Faster • 978-1-932096-41-5
Ronald Reagan: Destiny at His Side • 978-1-932096-65-1
Davy Crockett: Ever Westward • 978-1-932096-67-5
Milton Hershey: More Than Chocolate • 978-1-932096-82-8
Billy Graham: America's Pastor • 978-1-62486-024-9
Ben Carson: A Chance at Life • 978-1-62486-034-8
Louis Zamperini: Redemption • 978-1-62486-049-2
Elizabeth Fry: Angel of Newgate • 978-1-62486-064-5
William Wilberforce: Take Up the Fight • 978-1-62486-057-7
William Bradford: Plymouth's Rock • 978-1-62486-092-8
Ernest Shackleton: Going South • 978-1-62486-093-5
Benjamin Rush: The Common Good • 978-1-62486-123-9
Dwight Eisenhower: Supreme Commander • 978-1-62486-142-0
Frederick Douglass: The Right to Dignity • 978-1-62486-151-2
Winston Churchill: Resolute • 978-1-62486-153-6